Barcode at the back

D1593888

**ASPATORE
BOOKS**

About Aspatore Books
The Biggest Names in Business Books & More....
www.Aspatore.com

Aspatore Books has become one of the leading business book publishers in record setting time by publishing an all-star cast of C-level (CEO, CTO, CFO, COO, CMO) leaders from over half the Fortune 100 companies and other leading executives. Aspatore Books publishes the Inside the Minds, Bigwig Briefs, OneHourWiz and Aspatore Business Review imprints in addition to other best selling non-fiction books. Aspatore Books is focused on infusing creativity, innovation and interaction into the book publishing industry and providing a heightened experience for readers worldwide. Aspatore Books focuses on publishing traditional print books, while our portfolio company, Big Brand Books focuses on developing areas within the book-publishing world. Aspatore Books is committed to providing our readers, authors, bookstores, distributors and customers with the highest quality books, book related services, and publishing execution available anywhere in the world.

About Big Brand Books

Big Brand Books assists leading companies and select individuals with book writing, publisher negotiations, book publishing, book sponsorship, worldwide book promotion and generating a new revenue stream from publishing. Services also include white paper, briefing, research report, bulletin, newsletter and article writing, editing, marketing and distribution. The goal of Big Brand Books is to help our clients capture the attention of prospective customers, retain loyal clients and penetrate new target markets by sharing valuable information in publications and providing the highest quality content for readers worldwide. For more information please visit www.BigBrandBooks.com or email jonp@bigbrandbooks.com.

INSIDE THE MINDS

Inside the Minds:
Leading Advertisers

*Industry Leaders Share Their Knowledge on the
Future of Advertising, Marketing and
Building Successful Brands*

160101

**ASPATORE
BOOKS**

Published by Aspatore Books, Inc.

For information on bulk orders, sponsorship opportunities or any other questions please email sales@aspatore.com. For corrections, company/title updates, comments or any other inquiries please email info@aspatore.com.

First Printing, September 2001
10 9 8 7 6 5 4 3 2 1

ISBN 1-58762-054-5

Library of Congress Card Number: 2001118200

Cover design by Michael Lepera/Ariosto Graphics & James Weinberg

Material in this book is for educational purposes only. This book is sold with the understanding that neither any of the authors or the publisher is engaged in rendering legal, accounting, investment, or any other professional service.

This book is printed on acid free paper.

A special thanks to all the individuals that made this book possible.

Special thanks also to: Rinad Beidas, Kirsten Catanzano, Melissa Conradi and especially Ted Juliano

The views expressed by the individuals in this book do not necessarily reflect the views shared by the companies they are employed by (or the companies mentioned in this book). The companies referenced may not be the same company that the individual works for since the publishing of this book.

Inside the Minds:
Leading Advertisers

*Industry Leaders Share Their Knowledge on the
Future of Advertising, Marketing and
Building Successful Brands*

CONTENTS

CHANGE OR BE CHANGED

M T RAINEY

Young & Rubicam/
Rainey Kelly Campbell Roalfe

Co Chief Executive

Exciting Aspects of the Advertising Industry

From a personal point of view, the exciting aspect of our business is the sheer diversity of industries and companies that we get to work with. I may come into the same place of work most days - but in any one day I can be thinking about hugely diverse problems across a range of different kinds of businesses - from telecommunications to retail to toothpaste. Involvement with this wide range of industries and companies at various stages of their life cycles is endlessly fascinating. Believe it or not, no two problems are ever exactly the same - no matter how long you've been in the business - so there's always an element of novelty and challenge.

Also, the ability to make a difference to the outcome of something is always highly motivating. When you have a really great insight into a market or a brand that results in a new idea for that brand or a new way of thinking about that brand - that's very satisfying. It is this ability, power if you like, to influence the direction and therefore the success of a company that is always hugely rewarding.

Changes in the Advertising Industry

In the nineties, during the last recession, all of the laziness and complacency of advertising was stripped away by necessity. What has happened as a result of that, going into the next century, is that a much leaner and meaner industry has evolved which is more able to focus on it's core strengths and is more able to package and sell them to the market. Before that, advertising was working under a black box commission system, and was quite rightly accused of taking advantage of certain ingrained anachronistic structures in the industry. Those structures are largely now being superceded by much fairer and transparent industry practices. I think that's a good thing because it means that the agency business is becoming less commoditized and that value and contribution are more likely to be recognized financially.

I think advertising has become less God-like. It used to be the absolute lead discipline in most clients' marketing plans. Even though that is often still true, it doesn't represent quite the same centrifugal force that it used to in marketing. There are lots of other ways now that clients can communicate with consumers, and with the rise of consumer power, clients have realized that everything they do communicates - not just the "paid for" communications. The brand is perceived through all it's activities, not just it's advertising. So advertising has to be part of a much more holistic picture rather than at the top of a communications pyramid - or indeed the sheen you put on an otherwise lazy brand. Clients are increasingly looking for ideas that can belong to their brands, not just ideas that belong to the advertising for their brands.

The good thing about that for agencies is that I think they still possess the unique skill base for precisely that kind of "media neutral" thinking in the form of great account planners, enlightened account management and creative people who can rise above the craft skills of copywriting and art direction to more conceptual creativity about brands and markets. Clients still need the unique combination of insight and creativity that can transform a brand, and that's what agencies have always been about - it's just that now the ideas will have to reside above the level of pure advertising solutions.

The Effect of New Media on Advertising

Everything has been impacted by the Internet, broadband, and digital media. They add to the myriad ways in which ideas can be communicated and people can be communicated with. They also change the inherent psychological contract between the sender/vendor (brand) and receiver/consumer of messages. Ironically, the more diverse the channels become the more vital it is to have a central idea that becomes recognizably and uniquely yours. The more that people are able to access "perfect information" about every company or brand on the Internet, the more important it is that your brand be among the repertoire of brands they seek out or want to check out.

We should remember that brands developed originally as a shortcut to meaning were a necessary way to facilitate choice in the burgeoning consumer society. So, brands become even more important as "information" becomes ever more plentiful (i.e., on the Internet). I believe, however, that real brands require public affirmation, not just private appreciation and that they still have to be built and grown "offline".

The Importance of Ideas

Intellectual property is now more important in all businesses than virtually anything else. Advances in technology mean that companies cannot provide a long-term differentiating platform on the basis of a service or product difference alone. In six months, your competitor will have the same thing.

The tangible aspects of brands, products, and services are going to become more commoditized, and the intangible aspects of them are going to be what is most prized and valuable. Excellent products and services will be a necessary but insufficient condition for winning in the marketplace. Products can be copied, but ideas, once owned by and identified with brands, cannot so easily be dislodged. Intangible assets such as well-known and respected brands are going to become more important than ever.

Another reason why intellectual property is increasingly important is the explosion and fragmentation of media. There are so many ways that you can communicate with your customers now that almost everything is a medium. If you were to try and create original communications for every single medium starting from scratch it would be impractical and counterproductive. The more fragmented media is, the greater the requirement for a central linking and recognizable idea.

Keeping a Brand Fresh

The great folly of managing a brand is to only manage it in relation to it's own history. Quite a lot of brand owners become so obsessed with the iconography and history of their own brand that they see the future of the brand only in relation to where it has been. The reality is that all brands compete in a dynamic and open marketplace so if you don't change, and others do, then others inevitably change you. A "constant incremental" strategy is highly vulnerable in the face of a "radical innovation" strategy by competitors or new entrants. The history books are littered with big players who "didn't see it coming" because they weren't looking in the right place or were too complacent about their own position. The positioning of brands is always dynamic and always relative.

The biggest temptation is to be lazy and incremental rather than visionary and risk taking. A good example of this is Marks & Spencer in the UK which has seen a decline in recent years from a very dominant position in UK retailing. They were a hugely successful company, but they neglected what was going on around them and what other brands were doing in the marketplace. They neglected to appreciate the way that customers' choices and expectations were being changed or broadened by other retail experiences - because of course the volume impact of that was not felt immediately. Big brands will usually have the resources to fight back but they may spend several years and many millions doing so.

I often think that clients really underestimate the way broad market expectations are altered by visionary niche brands. Take First Direct in the banking market - many competitors wrote it off as a niche, and even though it is not a mainstream brand in volume terms, it totally redefined what consumers could expect their banks to provide and all the major players have now had to invest heavily in meeting those expectations. Similarly Virgin Atlantic in the airline market. It was a tiny airline which has grown to become an important player, but specifically that altered expectations of what was possible in a way that forced the big players to adapt.

So in managing a brand, it's important to remember that your brand is in a dynamic marketplace with other things moving around it, so change or be changed. Also, I believe you have to always see your brands relative to the leading edge of competition rather than just your near or mainstream competitors.

Tradition in a World Driven by Innovation

For some companies, heritage and tradition are key assets in both operations and communications. However, it would be important for companies to express those traditional values in a relevant and contemporary way. Values can remain traditional but communications must stay current. If a brand's communications start to look jaded or complacent, that will reflect badly on the brand. The job of the agency is to be on top of that issue - to keep the brand current and relevant in the culture through all it's communications - which does not preclude the expression of traditional values.

A Successful Campaign

More and more I find that unless your advertising is capturing the public interest, it is not really working hard enough. Advertising is very much a part of our public culture today - people are very literate about advertising and it's uses and the press writes about ads the way they would write about movies and TV programs. Campaigns that engage the public - that really get talked about in the pub, in newspapers, on chat shows or in chat rooms are really optimizing this new reality. If your advertising is not impinging on the culture in some way, it is probably too predictable and too similar to "all other advertising". It's a scientific fact that people process what is different at a much higher level of consciousness than what is expected. That word of mouth effect has incalculable value.

It used to be the case, certainly in the United State, that agencies could be broadly segmented into two groups: those that believed in " selling" advertising and those that believed in "creative" advertising. I believe that in observing how advertising works over the past twenty years we have learned that creativity is not an option - it is an imperative. In fact creativity is a prerequisite for effectiveness and success. Most agencies now would argue that they have an effectiveness culture.

Global Advertising

Of course it is possible to do global advertising - but I think it is virtually impossible to do global advertising that is equally effective in every market. Some advertisers take the view that the brand consistency promised by global advertising is worth the trade off.

Others take the view that it is more important to optimize the brand in each local or regional market to make sure that it is performing against local competition because the net result for the brand and business will be better.

In the late eighties and nineties we saw a huge swing towards international advertising as brands became preoccupied with globalization. In the new century we are seeing a significant move away from that with big multinational brands - even ones that are effectively identical everywhere (i.e. McDonald's, Coca Cola) - moving to a more devolved, market specific approach.

The Effect of New Technology on Broadcast Media

In spite of the boom and bust experience of the dot.com world, every company is still keen on learning how to use the Internet to optimize and grow their businesses. Very few, however, would consider the Internet as an alternative to mainstream media for building brands. Certainly the Internet offers a new channel for retail, customer communication and customer service, but brands and advertisers who abandon "broadcast" for "narrowcast" are taking a real risk. Brands still need to exist in the public marketplace - micro marketing is the sharp end of marketing but mass marketing is still the power end of marketing. The Internet is an unbelievable new medium - but it does different things well.

Budgeting for an Advertising Campaign

No matter how big a client's budget is, it's never big enough. With the management of any budget in advertising, you always have to make choices. The decision to do a little bit of everything is always a bad decision. Advertising can't do or say everything but it can do certain things really well and there are some things that only advertising can do. Defining and agreeing the role for advertising is the most important thing an agency and client will do together. You must be clear and honest about what you want the advertising to do and let other things do different parts of the marketing job (though ideally using the same central brand idea).

If you have a limited budget, it is much more incumbent to have advertising that is going to get talked about. That is an absolute mandate for small advertisers, and the great creative agencies of the world have built their reputations by doing just that. They started out small, but "famous advertising" turned them into big agencies. There is greater creative freedom typically allowed on smaller budgets, because small brands know that they have to do something that punches above their weight. Ironically, big advertisers don't tend to remember this as they can "buy" the weight - but creativity remains a key competitive advantage for any brand no matter what their size.

Compensation for Agencies

It occurred to me as a manager of an agency and after being in the business for a long time that traditional compensation methods were not designed to foster either mutual trust or profitability between clients and agencies. How agencies were being paid was not reflecting the quality of the work we did, either good or bad.

I do think the old commission system was highly iniquitous for both clients and agencies. In general, it undervalued the exceptional contributions of agencies to the fortunes of brands and it overpaid agencies for reaping commissions on media spends that had nothing to do with the quality or amount of work done. Certain agencies at certain times for certain brands have massively transformed the value of companies through clever thinking and great advertising campaigns. Because they have been trapped in the commission system they have been paid a relative pittance for doing that. On the contrary, agencies have often profited disproportionately from large investments in media that have not required similar investments in work, contribution or time.

The industry has now moved largely toward a more fee-based structure that is a more fair way to pay. Our agency in particular has a structure which charges basic resource fees, then also fees for the delivery and continued use of a brand idea. Our profit is built into the idea fee and is therefore contingent on delivery, which makes for much better partnerships with our clients.

The Dream Client

Rich, smart and with a sense of humor - or is that just my taste in men! Seriously though - I think agencies like working with clients who are open to the possibility of transformation. Advertising can be a lever for significant change in the fortunes of a brand or it can just be a cost to compete. Agencies can do their best work for clients who believe in the power of communication and who don't come with a blueprint for the answer. Agencies can add a huge amount to the intellectual capital of brands if they have the mandate to do so.

Discipline in the Industry

I think perhaps people outside the industry underestimate the amount of discipline that is inherent in the way agencies work, because it can often appear simply creative and chaotic. Working in a team requires a great focus on people skills and negotiating skills, both internally and with clients. Of course there's always constant monitoring and evaluation. There's always lots of research to refer to, use, conduct and act on at many different points in the process. And developing advertising to a copy date involves some pretty disciplined project management!

Decisions in advertising are not made in a haphazard way. Yes, there is an element of magic and serendipity in the process that is unquantifiable in advance - it is impossible to time it or legislate for it. A great idea is most likely to take the form of a Eureka moment within a disciplined process.

Creating the Environment for Creativity

A huge amount of it has to do with the physical

environment and geography you create. I worked with Chiat Day for ten years. When it came to understanding how agency people should work together they were real innovators. They created a fantastic and stimulating environment, which encouraged teamwork and creativity and broke down departmental politics. I now really believe that environment is critical to the ability to foster the right kind of discipline and the right kind of magic.

The environment also has a lot to do with the culture you create in the relationships between the agency and it's clients. If you have a partnership relationship with mutual respect, then that relationship can produce great results for both parties. Agencies that think in terms of having a valuable "product" rather than just providing a "service" are likely to end up being more valuable to their clients.

Creating a Client Relationship

You create that relationship by creating that kind of agency culture. To some extent, it is a self-determining process. If you run an agency with a strong set of beliefs, principles, and a particular view of advertising, then you will attract clients that are interested and respectful of that. If you are just a big factory for all kinds of clients and advertising, and don't have a particular view of how advertising works, then you are basically just a supermarket for different approaches and clients' relationships will be more variable and unpredictable. If you have a strong view of what it is that you do, your client relationships will self-select.

I think the culture of selling the ads has had its day. Really the agency has a product that is very valuable - and it is something that the clients can't do themselves. There has to be a mutual respect in the relationship and an opportunity for constructive debate and exchange of honest points of view. The client has to be able to be prepared to be surprised by the agency and the direction they want to take. There has to be give and take in the relationship. This old culture of salesmanship is really dangerous. There has to be a very high degree of mutual respect and a forum for debate that doesn't rest on this fallacy that you are always trying to sell something to them.

Becoming a Leader in Advertising

From an agency point of view, you have to stand for something, just like any brand.

As an individual, you have to be willing to go out there and have a point of view that isn't always popular or comfortable. I think that you also need a talent for advertising and you have to be passionate about the business.

To be a leader you have to care about the industry - it's practices and reputation, not just those of your own company. A leader will have the opportunity to shape the industry and should care about that.

Spotting Talent

You look for different things for different aspects of the business. What always catches my eye though is someone who is not afraid to stand up and say what they think. Whether they are right or wrong doesn't matter, someone with a bit of boldness and conviction always stands out.

Building a Successful Team

A team needs complementary skills. For a team to work, they need the same goal but different skills. They need to share the values but be good at different things and they should respect what the other team members are good at. If you have too many people in a company who do the same thing, it's not going to be as strong as a company with a more balanced skill set.

Valuable Skills for an Advertising Team

The core skills of account management are diplomacy, empathy, project management and the ability to understand the clients business. Planners need an ability to understand how advertising works and a curiosity about that. A planner who can describe a problem or an insight with passion and conviction and who has the ability to persuade is highly valuable. Creativity or an appreciation of it is a prerequisite in any of the disciplines. Creative thinking is as important as creative work.

The Future of Advertising

As media and channels become more fragmented, there will be even bigger demand for ideas that can transform brands and agencies that provide unique creative properties that go across the marketing mix.

More businesses will shake free of international alignments and experiment with smaller local agencies. The big multinational groups will respond by creating swat teams of entrepreneurship and talent within their agencies who create the "software" for clients and brands that the network manages and distributes.

There will be a rise in interest in Cause Related Marketing and the creation of Citizen Brands as companies are forced to confront their place in society as well as their place in the economy.

A native of Glasgow, M T (Mary Teresa) was a Founder and Managing Partner of Rainey Kelly Campbell Roalfe, which she built from scratch in 1993 to a top 20 agency in 6 years. The agency was aquired by Y&R in '99 to merge with its London office. She is now Co Chief Executive of

Rainey Kelly Campbell Roalfe / Y&R, the sixth biggest Agency in the UK and now part of WPP.

A graduate of Glasgow University, M T is an honorary member of the Account Planning Group and a Visiting Professor at the University of Glasgow Business School. She is also a Trustee of the innovative charities Pilotlight and Timebank, as well as a Trustee of the thinktank Demos. She is a regular speaker and publisher on communications and media industry issues both in the UK and abroad.

RALLYING THE TROOPS

ERIC ROSENKRANZ

Grey Global Group

President & CEO Asia Pacific

Enjoyable Aspects of Advertising

I began my advertising career in the United States and worked there for seven years, climbing rapidly up the corporate ladder in traditional advertising. I decided I wanted to try something different, so I asked for an international assignment. Two days later I was on a plane to Mexico

That was in 1982.

It launched my career in international advertising, a career that successfully continues through today.

During my career, the opportunity to move around the world and work with different cultures has been a motivation and reward for me.

If you take everything that's been said about trying to understand a difficult consumer, you can multiply that by 100-fold when you have to work with a consumer from a different culture.

I am fortunate to have the opportunity to try and figure out what is going on in the minds of consumers all over the world. In addition, I am privileged to work with people across many countries who are all from different cultures and backgrounds. They don't think as I do, they don't emote as I do. I love it. It challenges me every day, making me consider, "Am I thinking about this issue in an appropriate, creative way, or is there a different and perhaps better way to approach it?"

I pretty much have reinvented myself every three years for the past twenty years, trying to change jobs every three years. I have remained within the same company, yet engineered my career so that it was highly dynamic. This keeps me from "going stale". That's another thing I like about advertising - it affords the ability to try many different things. In the past 20 years, I have moved seven times and lived in six different countries, holding six different jobs. There has been no time to stagnate, no time to stop learning.

The industry excites me because it is a blend of business and creativity. You can be a businessman and work closely with finance and financials. This appeals to the left side of the brain, to rationality. At the same time, you are dealing with art, creativity and the intangible. You are trying to convince people to do something different. That appeals to the non-rational right brain of an executive. That blend between art and business has always attracted me to the industry - and held my fascination.

Creating a Brand

The purpose of advertising is to convince the consumer to take an action. It may be to buy something for the first time, buy it again, switch brands, use a product or service more frequently...any one of a hundred different actions. Fundamentally, however, we are trying to get a prospect, existing customer, or lapsed customer to do something.

The way we achieve this is by creating a brand. A brand is different than a product. A product is a set of physical characteristics. A brand adds something intangible, and highly valuable, on top of those physical characteristics. Take Mercedes and BMW, for example. For all intents and purposes they are identical cars. They are highly engineered, very expensive, and very luxurious. Although the engineers in Germany would disagree, to the average driver, there is really no difference between them mechanically.

But, there are people who are passionate about Mercedes who would never drive a BMW, and vice versa. There is something about the "aura" and appeal of each car that makes their owner feel very differently about it. The brand that is created is much more than the sum of its parts, that is, more than what the car is about physically. The brand creates the real value.

Consider blue jeans. Many blue jeans look alike. But tell a polo wearer to switch to Armani and they won't do that. People wear the brand, the label, not the material. Can you tell one blue jean from another? Not really, but if you are wearing Polo or Armani, you are making a statement about yourself.

Now, none of this is particularly revolutionary. The key point is, if what we are trying to do is create a brand, in reality the client doesn't own that brand. The client has created a product.

The advertising agency doesn't own the brand. The agency creates the medium to communicate information about the brand. The person who really creates the brand is the consumer. It happens via the stimulus the client produces in terms of a product, and that the agency creates through the words and images of its advertising. Then the consumer adds his or her own values and perspective. The creation of the brand is really a three-way exchange between client, agency, and consumer. But in the end, the consumer is the only one who truly "owns" that brand. And their ongoing interaction with the brand evolves and redefines it over time.

What do we do when we work with a client for the first time? First, we try to understand the product. As mentioned, the product is more than just a set of physical characteristics, and a good client will not only understand this, but also have a vision for what they believe their brand should stand for or represent beyond its physical properties. Simultaneously, we try to understand what the client is all about, because the best advertising and branding comes from a long-term relationship between the client and the agency. When we are meeting a client for the first time, we are not looking to be their marketing partner for the next six months; we are looking at the next twenty years. We want to know the vision the client has for his or her brand as far into the future as possible. How does that client plan to evolve and develop that product over time?

We also have to get inside that client's thinking to understand the types of communications he or she wants to use to reach the consumer and why. While there is no question that the client understands his or her product better than anyone else, we often work with clients to evolve their thinking. The fundamental things we are looking for with a client in a first meeting is his or her understanding of the product and an understanding of their vision for the type of brand they would like to create. We then take our knowledge of the consumer and begin the process of investigating, conceptualizing, and creating recommendations for the brand. Consumers react to these communications, sometimes creating feedback that leads to new recommendations, thereby continuing the process - their process - of creating the brand. Full circle.

Ads that Go Wrong

A very prosaic explanation could be that some advertising doesn't understand the consumer and so communicates the wrong benefit, or values. The pitfall is trying too hard and therefore turning off the consumer. We see this a lot in purely emotional advertising. Let's say you're creating a beer ad. There is very little product message that one can communicate, you are simply selling an emotion. Often the advertiser tries so hard to be funny, amusing, or sexy that the consumer shakes his head and walks away in disgust, because the ad is unbelievable, or even offensive. There are numerous examples of beer campaigns that have failed for these reasons.

Another time advertising often fails is when a purely rational approach is used, where an advertiser has one message and proceeds to drum that message home until the consumer is tired of it. A lot of packaged good advertising falls into this category. It is completely rational and provides no room for an emotional appeal, no opportunity to build an emotional bond with the consumer. That also tends to turn consumers off. Campaigns that fail because they do not understand the consumer haven't really listened to the consumer. Consequently, the campaign sends them a message that they are either not ready to receive, or unwilling to receive.

The best advertising is based on true understanding and insight into the consumer and communicates in a way designed to appeal to both his or her rational side, as well as emotional side. That's what makes advertising so difficult to develop and measure. Deciding whether we have communicated rational points is easy, it is the emotional side that is toughest and requires great effort, insight and experience

One crucial, yet infrequently discussed aspect of our business is media. Media planning and buying is critical because no matter how good a campaign may be, it is useless if it does not reach the consumers we would like it to. Conversely, a bad campaign with excellent media planning can be equally useless - and in fact, damaging. We have a number of highly specialized media executives who combine both a keen intelligence and knowledge of the business with sophisticated tools used to calculate the optimal media for any given ad, the most desirable programs or sections within that media, and optimal number of times the ad should run.

To illustrate the point about the value of smart advertising combined with smart media planning and buying, consider that an average commercial might run 10 or 20 times on television. Think about it: How many times has a television commercial come on, and you instantly think "I have seen this ad before, it is awful, and I am not going to watch it again" Zap! You reach for your remote control. How many times has the opposite happened? You are watching a program, a commercial comes on, and even though you've already seen it, you love it and think it's hilarious. You call your partner or friend to come in and say, "Come watch this ad. It's great"!

If we have smart people trying to figure out how to efficiently maximize a budget based on how many times a commercial goes on the air, yet the consumer is turned off by the second airing, we might have wasted up to 95% of the clients budget. The opposite thing happens if the consumer loves the commercial and invites other people to come watch it. Then, we are in effect, multiplying the value of that ad or campaign. Not only are more people viewing the advertising, they are viewing it more intently, and are more likely to receive the intended message.

The pitfall is in turning the consumer off to the point that they are not paying any attention to your message. This is a concern because, again, you have just wasted ninety five percent of your budget, either because the ad is irrelevant to the consumer or perhaps even offensive. It's easy to go wrong when creating campaigns. It's tough to do everything right. But when everything does work to perfection, and sales soar, it makes all the sweat worthwhile.

Measuring the Success of a Campaign

Have you heard of reading tea leaves?

It's a bit like that.

A lot of times, someone comes to me with an ad, and asks me if it is a good ad. I say I can't answer that question because I have to know what the ad's objectives are.

There is no good or bad advertising, there's just advertising that does or does not meet its objectives.

You can have a brilliant ad that is creating trial, but if your objective is to get people to buy the brand over and over again, then creating trial is not going to do that. Before we develop any ad, we try to figure out what our objectives for that ad is - what we are trying to accomplish. Then we can measure that ad based on whether we think it accomplishes those goals or not. To simply ask if sales went up is not enough. It is virtually impossible today to measure the sales of a product and relate that completely to advertising. There are so many other variables: distribution, pricing, competitive activity, etc. To hold all of the other variables constant and to just say that advertising built the business is extremely difficult. We can measure whether advertising has prompted more people to try a product. Maybe we want awareness or people to remember the product. That can be measured too.

Let's use cars as an example. Advertising doesn't cause somebody to buy a car, it simply can cause someone to walk into the showroom. A salesperson (at least a good one) can then make the sale to the prospective buyer. It could be that we define the success of car advertising as how many people walked into the showroom. That's measurable.

The short answer to the question is that we can only measure the effectiveness of an ad if we have determined before we create the ad what the objectives are.

Favorite Advertising Tools

I don't have a favorite advertising medium. That implies that all advertising media accomplish the same thing and you just choose one because you like it more than the other. The truth is, you need to choose the media based on what you plan to accomplish. There are times when a running a simple newspaper campaign is the most beneficial approach as opposed to undertaking a million dollar television campaign. This is often a misleading issue. Many people in the industry like working with television because it combines the sound of radio, with the visual aspect of print, and the motion of movies. In fact, many people in advertising are actually frustrated cinematographers or directors which is part of the problem.

Personally, I can get as much joy out of a single-line, black and white print ad in a newspaper if it accomplishes its goal. To me, it's all about the end result... it's all about the accomplishment of the goal.

The Next Big Advertising Medium

I don't think it exists. I am not a negative person and I'm certainly not a futurist. But as soon as a new media comes along, we will understand it and it will be skillfully incorporated into our toolbox. We have no way of predicting the future. Will something come along to revolutionize the industry? It's hard to say. Everybody in the 1990's was talking about the Internet revolutionizing the world, and that was perhaps the biggest collapse of an industry in recent history. Yet, we know it's an important medium, albeit one that works best when used in combination with other media.

I don't really foresee anything coming. If a "killer app" does come along, we will all quickly evaluate it and figure out how to use it. When you look in the past hundred years, although there have been tremendous inventions, how many have revolutionized the world? Maybe the telephone and the airplane. There hasn't been that many. I am someone who doesn't believe in revolution as much as evolution.

Opportunities for Advertisers Going Forward

There are two main challenges that will provide an opportunity for our industry to advance the state of the art.

Developing a Better Understanding of Consumers

The biggest challenge facing advertisers is understanding the consumer's mind. It is not always easy to understand what the consumer wants. Often, they are unable to tell you what they want by articulating it. It's often a gut feeling they have, or a series of words or feelings we need to help them express.

Imagine yourself working in the car industry during the 1950's when everyone was driving a stick shift. If you were to ask a consumer what future innovation they would like, you couldn't expect them to say they would like an automatic transmission. Consumers can't invent things they've never heard of.

You have to ask the consumer what problems they have in driving a car, and then the consumer may say they hate the constant shifting. Then as a manufacturer, you might have the idea to develop an automatic transmission. Now, that's less of an advertising issue and more of a product design issue but it illustrates the point that very often a consumer cannot articulate what they want. It's then up to the advertising agency to present that new idea in a way to make it appealing.

Here's another problem in understanding the consumer. The consumer may not always answer correctly to a direct question. Back to the car industry. If you ask a consumer directly what he or she wants in a car, they will say they want safety, miles to the gallon, and durability. If you ask them what their neighbor wants, they might say that their neighbor wants a sexy hot car that looks cool and goes fast. That may be what the individual wants for himself, but they often can't or won't answer the question directly because they are embarrassed. So, as marketers, we have to phrase the question in a different way. By the way, I didn't make these examples up; they are classic examples in our industry of the consumer not really telling you what they want.

Our job is to understand what the consumer wants because advertising is all about convincing the consumer to do something - to try a new product, switch to a new product, or use a product repeatedly over time. Again, advertising is trying to get the consumer to change his or her behavior in some way. To do this, we need to truly understand the consumer, sometimes even better than they may understand themselves, at least consciously. To understand the consumer we need to figure out the consumer, and the consumer's mind is a very dangerous and subtle thing.

The industry has a major opportunity in figuring out ways to understand the consumer better. Let's go back fifty years. In the 1950's, the industry invented something called the focus group. This was an extremely valuable innovation. Today, we use focus groups for a wide range of purposes including copy and creative testing, pre- and post-campaign testing, gauging reactions to new products, and more. The original focus group had a bunch of consumer sitting around the table, and a bunch of ad men standing behind a curtain. Now we have sophisticated two-way mirrors and other techniques.

But somebody had to invent the concept of getting consumers together to talk about what they want. We've come a long way since then, and the industry is constantly inventing new ways to understand the consumer. Some of these things work and some of them don't. But again, that's a golden opportunity for our industry now and in the future.

For example, I believe that it is primarily emotions, rather than cognition, that drive decisions about brands. We're working on a research technique that measures the emotional proximity between an individual and a brand, what we call the measure of intimacy, based on such factors as familiarity, relevance, accessibility, affinity, identification and desirability. This gives us a much more finely calibrated insight into the consumers we are targeting for any given purpose.

Critics of our industry will say that we try to manipulate the consumer. The fact is that we are not that smart! We are not clever enough to be able to figure out the consumer well enough to "manipulate" them. If we could, we'd all be millionaires.

New Media Development

A second area of opportunity is in the development of new media. To illustrate this, let's take a brief look at the history of advertising over the past hundred years. Modern advertising traces back to the 1880's. When advertising first started, the first media vehicles were newspapers. In the early 1900's, you had newspapers, radio in the 1920's, and television in the 1950's. What happened when each of the new media came along was that everybody said it was revolutionary and would change the industry dramatically. We didn't understand how the new media worked. We needed to hire specialist people and set them aside in a distinct division or company, and do nothing but focus on these new media and their implications for marketers and consumers. When commercial television evolved, there were companies and advertising agencies that did nothing but television advertising. After a while, each new media became integrated within the mainstream. In a classic advertising agency today, you don't have someone who specializes in radio or television - it all works together

We see this phenomenon happening in the last few years with the Internet. When the Internet exploded in the late 1990's, everybody said it would revolutionize advertising, and there needed to be special companies that specialized exclusively in interactive advertising. They argued that all other media were virtually (no pun intended) dead. I was quoted in a major journal as saying, "That's all stuff and nonsense. What's going to happen with the Internet is exactly the same thing that happened to television, radio, and the newspaper. We will set up separate companies, focus on it, and try to learn it. Eventually however, it will integrate within the mainstream".

That's exactly what has happened. Now all of the companies that are specializing in Internet advertising are collapsing. The Internet is becoming another tool in the toolbox of different media that we have. The opportunity that we have going forward is that there will be more new media that enable new means of communications, new ways of interacting with consumers. I have no idea what the new media is going to be like in ten year's time. Is it broadband or WAP or G3? I have no idea. But I know there will be something. This is one of our constant challenges - taking the new media, learning about them, and then integrating them into our existing arsenal for maximum effect.

Changes in Advertising

It's become harder and easier at the same time. It's easier because we understand the consumer more. It's harder because the consumer has become more complex.

The consumer of the year 2000 is much more sophisticated than the consumer of the 1950's. While we have techniques to understand the consumer better, we are dealing with a more complex, better-educated and more demanding consumer, in short, a consumer who is more difficult. One of the reasons that the consumer is more difficult to deal with is that the consumer is attacked by more messages daily. A commonly quoted figure in Europe states that the average person is bombarded daily by an astounding 13,000 messages a day. These are huge numbers, significantly larger than those of even ten years ago. We are dealing with a more sophisticated consumer who not only is bombarded by more messages, but who has more brand choices than ever before. (How many more detergents or cars do you have to choose from today compared to fifty years ago?) So, the number of media, media messages and brand choices are on the increase, making the challenge even more interesting. While our techniques have become better and more sophisticated, and we have more weapons at our disposal, it's more difficult to attract the consumer now. It's become simultaneously easier and harder.

In my viewpoint, that's the second main challenge in the industry today. And this is what makes working in our industry so exciting - it is never static, and it never gets any easier.

Exciting Aspects of Internet and Technology

There are three aspects that particularly excite me.

One is depth of sale. Many of us in the industry have been frustrated by the limited amount of communication that can be achieved in a thirty second commercial or even a one page magazine ad. The Internet allows an infinite amount of brand communication as long as one has managed to entice the consumer to be interested in it - and one continues to communicate with them in a manner that is relevant to their needs.

Second, the ability to talk "one-to-one" with the consumer. Advertising has traditionally been called a mass-market media. You put a message out there and you are talking to millions of people at the same time, in the same way.

Traditionally, direct marketing or a direct mail piece has been used for one-to-one communication so we can identify what a customer's interests are and tailor our communications to address those interests in a personalized manner that we try to make as relevant as possible to each individual. And by continuing to build the dialog, we can garner customer input along the way and tailor the process for each customer as necessary. Yet, traditional off line direct marketing efforts can be time consuming and fairly costly.

The Internet allows interactive communication where we can send a consumer a message, he or see can send it back, we can refine it, and via that refinement technique and the constant to and fro, we can find out what's right for that consumer and try to convince them to buy our product.

While based on exactly the same premise as direct mail, the Internet takes one-to-one communication a step further through its provision of immediacy and speed, enhanced targeting and relationship building capabilities through the formation of an ever evolving database - in turn enabling true, customer relationship management, enhanced cost efficiencies, and arguably, overall, greater effectiveness.

The Internet doesn't replace any of our tools, it supplements them and adds functionality. The third thing that really excites me about the Internet is its use as a tool in combination with other media. The speed and ease with which we can communicate in a customized way with consumers is a huge advantage. For example, the best media we have ever discovered for creating a brand is television advertising. But if I have conveyed a message via television advertising, I may have only planted a seed in your head, not prompted you to take an action. The Internet is not a good tool for creating a brand. However, it is an excellent means of calling a consumer to action, converting them to becoming a customer, and building a relationship with that customer over time to ensure a loyal, long-term relationship.

For example, let's say we have convinced you that you are really interested in a BMW. Now you are surfing the Internet, and a banner ad pops up about BMW. The idea was already in your head, and all you have to do is click on that link. It takes you to a site where you can then see a 3D picture of a BMW and see the product specs. The communications process builds from there, beginning with the possibility of purchase or conversion to after sales servicing, accessory sales, new model information based on that customer's interest, and, in an ideal world, preferred prices.

I am fascinated that the actual call to action comes after the branding message has been created through another medium. This supports my belief that great brands are not built through just one media, but through a combination of media that are well orchestrated all at the same time. That's what I like about the Internet. It allows us to do something the other media can't. If you've got a toolbox with a hammer, screwdriver, and pliers, now you've got a new tool that does something different.

The art and science of communication is knowing how to use these tools in the optimal combination to achieve a marketing objective in the most effective and efficient way possible. This begins by leveraging brand intelligence and consumer insights with planning to select the best tools for the job at hand. Once that's been done, I think it's critical that the executive with ownership of the primary communications discipline - whether it's advertising, PR, or one-to-one relationship marketing - lead the process of orchestrating the portfolio of communications.

The Future of Advertising

I can't predict how things are going to change over the next five years. However, I do see a disturbing trend that I believe will profoundly affect our business and adversely so unless we correct it. That trend revolves around people and unfortunately, money.

If a company manufactures soap for example, they must purchase chemicals for making the soap, factories to make it, and warehouses for its storage prior to distribution. Those items, among others, constitute their cost of goods.

In an advertising agency, our intellectual capital and primary cost of goods is our people. They are our ingredients, our factory, and our warehouse.

It's this simple: The more income we have, the higher the caliber of the people we can hire - quality people who can intelligently identify and tackle our client's challenges and generate effective solutions. Yet, there is a very clear trend in our industry toward reduced fees from our clients. Agencies fees have been sharply reduced in the past ten years and this pace is accelerating. It may well get worse before it gets better. We no longer have the money to attract the brightest people in the industry. Several years ago, people left our industry in droves for the Internet because venture capitalists threw money at them in bundles. Many of our best and brightest young stars defected to dot.coms. This became a huge "brain drain".

Sadly, I predict a gloomy future for advertising at least in the immediate future if we no longer are able to attract the best talent. We simply don't have the money to pay them anymore. In the end, this will rebound on our clients. Without the best minds to attack our client's problems, advertising will suffer, decline in quality and efficacy, and consequently, clients will see declines in their sales.

Client cutbacks on agency remuneration will come back to haunt them. This is an extremely serious threat now and into the future. While this may sound self-serving, I firmly believe that people are the future of our industry. We must figure out a way to re-attract the best people or we will not have the talent to compete.

Keeping an Edge

I walk the streets. Sure, I can say I read everything that I can get my hands on, go to industry conferences, and talk to other professionals. We all do that. I travel 80% of the time. Whenever I go to a new country or market I go into the streets and stores to try and talk to people in the shops.

Recently, I was in Beijing and I arranged on a Sunday to go to the house of a typical lower class consumer. I just sat in their house for an hour and looked in their kitchen, bathroom, and cupboards. It may seem strange for a CEO-level executive to do that, but that's how I can try to deeply understand what is going on in a country, and how people in that country live, think and feel. I am not going to figure that out staying in five star hotels.

When I go to India, I walk in the back streets and eat in the local restaurants. I try to communicate whenever possible to the people in the streets. That's how I like to keep my edge. This industry is about understanding people. You need to go where the people are.

Becoming a Leader

I always picture a general in the American Civil War when people ask me about leadership. He's got five thousand men in blue or gray uniforms behind him. There is a hill, and the enemy is on the other side. He takes out his sword and yells "Charge!" and goes running up the hill.

The question is: Are those five thousand men going to follow him or not? They could charge up the hill, or decide not to. If they make the latter choice, then that General is all by himself, waving his silly sword, and his men are down below having a cup of coffee.

To me, leadership is about creating a vision and communicating it powerfully. Having the ability to set a goal and objective is important, but you also need to communicate it. You must be able to convince others to take up your cause as passionately as you do yourself. Many people who want to be leaders are able to create a meaningful or relevant vision, but are unable to get anybody to come along with them. Inevitably, this is because they are not able to communicate persuasively.

One can see many examples of this in the business world. We have learned of several CEO's who have been asked to retire from their boards in the past few years. These are all incredibly intelligent, talented executives who are able to develop or generate a vision, but unable to rally their teams, including their boards, behind them.

Other executives are really strong team players, who are capable of generating a following, but who are not able to generate a compelling vision. In other words, the individual doesn't know where he or she is going. What's the point of having people follow you if you don't know where you want them to go?

I have always felt that leadership is the dual ability of being able to create and articulate a vision and to mobilize people to work with you to make that vision a reality. Once you have the vision, having empathy in being able to create a team and get that team working together for a common goal is really what leadership is all about. It's what I have always tried, although not always successfully, to do.

Recently, I held a regional meeting of all of our CEO's in Asia Pacific where I am currently working. I presented my vision for the region and a six-point plan for accomplishing that vision. That's a fairly standard agenda item for any leader holding a regional conference. Shortly afterward, I visited our office in Malaysia. The CEO there asked me to address the entire staff. We have two hundred people in our Malaysian office, ranging from secretaries and mail boys, to senior executive staff. I gave them the identical presentation I gave to the CEO's two weeks earlier. I sat down with the chief executive down to the office boy and told them our vision for the region and the six steps we would take to get there. I did that because I felt that if I was expecting people to accomplish something, they needed to know what I wanted them to accomplish. I couldn't just ask people to come in every day and work from nine to five without knowing what they were trying to achieve.

I received a tremendous response to my efforts. People didn't come to me directly because I don't think they would have felt comfortable doing so. But I heard a lot of feedback later that people were amazed at the presentation, and had never heard a CEO of a region give a vision statement like that before to the "rank and file". One woman, a secretary, who was on her first day of a job, said she was astounded that the President of her company was talking to her this openly.

That was my way of conveying my vision and making it their vision, by explaining it, bringing it life, and rallying people to work behind it. While I didn't do it to be self-serving, I also know that those two hundred people will now work diligently and passionately for the next year because they feel part of a bigger whole, a whole that will ensure a better future for our company and for each of them.

As President - Asia Pacific for Grey Worldwide, Eric is the first executive in the history of Grey Global Group to hold this position on two continents, having also been head of Grey Worldwide in Latin America. With ten years in Europe prior to his Latin America post, he is the company's first executive to have held senior positions in all three international divisions of the company. He brings to the job 26 years of experience in international marketing communications.

Prior to his current position, Eric headed up Grey Worldwide in Latin America from January, 1997 until June, 2000. Additional highlights of his tenure included the profitable restructuring of agencies in Argentina, Brazil, Mexico and Peru which also saw the introduction of new, innovative management teams. His strong emphasis on creativity resulted in Grey Worldwide companies winning more awards than ever before, and his commitment to integrated communications enabled the company to expand more quickly into Direct Marketing, Promotion, Public Relations, and Interactive Marketing.

63

THE FUTURE OF ADVERTISING: INVITATION ONLY, NO REGRETS

BOB BRENNAN

Leo Burnett Worldwide

President

Advertising Changes Over the Past Few Years

The advertising industry is transitioning from a focus on mass communications to one-on-one communication. Our population is swiftly evolving, and there is not one homogenous approach to communicating. A good part of the population grew up in and is most comfortable in the Age of Intrusion; i.e. consumers receive a message whether they want to or not. They have no control over when or how the message is given to them.

Another segment of the population is experiencing the Age of Invitation. These people are in control; they receive messages on their terms. While anyone born before 1980 grew up in the Age of Intrusion, today's kids are growing up in the Age of Invitation. The Age of Invitation was precipitated by an altered communications landscape. Marketers who are advertising to different targets but who only communicate on the basis of Intrusion won't appeal to those targets being weaned on the mode of Invitation. The industry has not come to grips with this dynamic yet.

Using Personal Information About Individual Consumers

Right now personal information is being thought about from a perspective of intrusion. As an industry we seek information that will enable us to intrude on the consumer in some way to inspire action. What we need to pursue as an industry is respect and engagement. Building a relationship and a partnership with a customer is imperative. We should only have or use information that the consumer wants us to have or use. And instead of asking, "How can I use information to better intrude on you?" we should ask, "How can I use information to better engage you?" Of course, all this begins with asking the right questions.

If marketers could only say to me, "Bob Brennan, tell us what you're into and we'll construct an environment that's right for you", and I could say back to them, "I never want to see another personal hygiene or laundry detergent ad in my life. But I am really into specific car models, the latest Cell phones or PDAs (personal digital assistants)". Then if ads for those types of products would be all I saw when I turned on my television or picked up my magazine, they would be interacting with me from personal information that drives engagement. If a typical media company can sell media on prime time television, CPM (cost per thousand homes) might get the message into a home for two cents. As an individual, it might be worth two dollars to get into my home if the entry was based on engagement as opposed to intrusion. This is heresy, of course, because it would lead to a fundamental disruption in the economics of the industry. And it seems no one's willing to go down that path. Very soon we will have to, because we owe it to our clients to create a better return on their investment. I contend that spending two dollars on a specific number of households to engage strong potential buyers in a meaningful exchange is a much better investment than spending two cents to spray an irrelevant message across a mass market.

Goals for a Successful Advertising Campaign

A successful campaign invites and entices, while growing a clients' business. It lures a consumer into its message by virtue of its relevance and meaning to the individual. And because it connects with and embraces buyers, it has real potential to transform them into believers. That more than anything is where real business results originate - in the buyers who are passionate believers in the brands they buy.

Establishing a Successful Advertising Campaign

Get in the face of the customer. Discover in the brand the aspect or attribute that the buyer can truly believe in. Get the sale. Go beyond the sale. Inspire advocacy. Demonstrate how the product or brand can enhance the way a person lives or works. Once you discover the promise of the brand, you must find a compelling message and media through which to deliver it. You must craft communication that drives the behavior to achieve the ultimate goals of the brand, and do so in a measurable way.

Examples of Campaigns That Stick Out From the Rest

Superior creativity causes campaigns to stand out. An example is an Altoids ad I noticed on the back cover of Mad Magazine called "Spy Vs Spy", which ties right in with the media vehicle. Brilliant creativity! Talk about an invitation. This ad says to people who have a unique perspective, "Hey, I'm a mint with a curious perspective and I'm right here where you live and play". It engaged me, bringing me right back to my youth.

Right Amount to Spend on Advertising

As much as it takes to make the connection with our target. There is no standard equation that universally captures this challenge.

A lot of people try to determine formulas. I've been at this for over 20 years, and I've found you have to test different scenarios in the marketplace and look at different industries. Some industries determine ad spending as a percentage of sales, where they spend .02 percent on advertising. Then you have others who spend 20% on advertising.

The opportunity today is to go into many marketplaces and discreetly measure different spending levels and approaches to determine what's working. I think we can get away from the old adage "I know 50% of my advertising budget is being wasted, I just don't know which 50%". The industry today can deliver far more precision than that, but we have to approach it differently.

Favorite Advertising Tools to Use When Cost is No Option

The tools are as varied as the brands and opportunities. A great tool is disruption: the big, the bold, and the unusual - like using street theater to deliver a compelling message. I also like dramatic creative unseen before like the use of email and digital technology to deliver a message. I remember a brilliant anti-Heroin campaign that came out of Singapore that was simply a viral email message that had no money behind it. People forwarded the email and, when it was opened, it displayed the word "Quit" on the computer screen. Every time you put your cursor on the word, it jumped to another location on the screen. Eventually the point was made that this is what it's like to be addicted; you can't get control of your life. I like things that inspire me, entertain me, and give me something to aspire to.

Clarifying Client's Advertising Objectives

Ask clients what they fundamentally want the advertising to do. Why do they want to spend money? What do they expect in return? Asking questions are the first step, listening to the answers is equally important.

If the client can identify concise answers to the questions, then you can work with them to identify the barriers that obstruct their objectives. The next step is to start drilling through the barriers. This process is essential and revealing. Sometimes the barriers have nothing to do with marketing communications. They might be related to distribution or a retail relationship problem. Sometimes at the end of the day what most motivates the client is Wall Street - the value of the company and the value of its stock. Getting at these issues is the first step in establishing an objective you can work toward.

Maintaining a Consistent Message in All Media

You search for a big idea - a fundamental truth that's going to motivate, inspire and drive consumer behavior - and then you communicate that big idea consistently across all communication practices.

Utilizing Different Media Yet Maintaining a Campaign's Core Message

Every brand has a promise. It has attributes that remain true. A brand telling its promise is like a person making a promise. Consistency is critical. If you betray your essence, your customers will find you out and they will lose faith. Our role is to find the true promise of a brand, then deploy and preserve it across all media. To some extent, we are the keepers of the brand. We have the authority and accountability to preserve the integrity of the brand wherever it comes in contact with its customer. It might sound like a big restriction, but it is really very liberating. If you can capture the essence of a brand, and you approach it with the right amount of passion and innovation, you can bring it to life across a broad palette of media. Consider a brand like Heinz. It has a personality. It is irreverent, but fun. It is young and passionate about taste and food. No matter where you might run into this brand - on the store shelf, on the Internet, on a high school textbook cover, in an email, on television, or in a magazine - you always experience the same personality. That's how trust is built. That's how brands are built.

Breaking Through With a Clear Brand That People Will Remember

You must understand your consumers and their behavior. You must comprehend just how to engage them, and then create an innovative message with power - one with unusual creativity that the market hasn't seen before, that breaks through and wins relative to the competition. If you don't reach them with a relevant message, you will be dismissed. People don't invite strangers in that often. The same principle holds true for brilliant, breakthrough brands.

New Technologies Besides the Internet That are Making an Impact on Advertising

New technology like Tivo and Replay TV, if properly used, can have a huge impact on marketing and advertising. I am very much interested in precisely understanding today's younger generation and how they engage and consume on their terms. There are certain aspects of how they multitask: being on the Web while there's a CD in the computer and TV on in the background. I want to understand how they interact in that whole milieu and how they derive fun and inspiration out of it.

Digital communications and broadband are currently redefining the direction of our industry and our capacity for one-on-one marketing.

In the not-too-distant future (and I'd like to be at the forefront of this), someone will create kiosk programs in cities where we will be able to download a digital image on street corners and change it instantly, breaking through the barriers of the out-of-home medium. I bet this comes more out of Europe than the U.S. I think there are revolutionary breakthroughs in the offing that will create great opportunities for marketers and media companies once an economic model based on Invitation develops.

New TV Technologies

New TV technologies that allow consumers to skip over commercial breaks definitely have our attention. More than anything, they reveal the frailty of the Intrusion philosophy. We need to change the industry dynamic and ask consumers, "How can we give you messages you want to receive?" We need to craft messages so compelling, the viewers will elect them into their environment. This is a lot of pressure. And it's going to intensify. Technology will be advanced in a way that continues to enable people to avoid what they don't want to see or hear. If it doesn't, the very busy, over-programmed consumer population will revolt.

We are already seeing this revolt with DVD movies. The entertainment industry has encoded DVD players and the DVD itself so that people can't avoid the FBI warning. On a VCR they can fast forward over it. People are already resentful that they have to watch the FBI warning over and over on DVDs. It remains to be seen how the industry will respond. The worst thing movie studios could do is employ that technology to make people watch the previews they put on DVDs. That would be going absolutely in the wrong direction. As far as advertising goes, our approach must be to present people with something so compelling, they will not hit the fast-forward button.

Enticing Consumers to Interact With Advertisements

What is critical to having a marketing campaign that works is a fusion of message and medium. Years ago, we were in a business where 90 percent of a marketer's success came from having the right message; the business was all about creativity. Today the mass market is non-existent and every individual interacts with messages uniquely. The message and how it's delivered are equally important. The most effective marketing campaigns in the future will have a great marriage of media thinking, creative thinking and customer thinking to engage and surround a consumer, and on his or her terms.

Advertising on the Internet: The Right and Wrong

"Nesting" is the right thing to do on the Internet. That means associating content with places where the right customers want to go, and doing so in a compelling manner that will make people want to interact with it. A good example would be putting brand content for a new Nintendo game on a Nickelodeon or Cartoon Network website in a way that engages the people that visit that website.

I think banner advertising will never work because it is fundamentally inconsistent with the dynamics of the medium. The Internet is all about individual control, and Intrusion is never going to work in that medium. That's why banner ads have response rates lower than FSI/coupon offers in newspapers. I've long believed that services like Yahoo! would crash because they followed the path the broadcast networks took rather than learning what Ted Turner did with CNN - that two revenue streams are always better than one. Media companies that have advertising and subscriptions as two different revenue streams will beat the networks someday unless the networks change their business models. Advertising alone is not going to be a primary medium on the Internet because it is inconsistent with the dynamic of the medium, which is all about engagement versus control.

A Global World and the Impact on Advertising

Marketers continue to search for global campaigns that communicate a universal truth across language and cultural borders because it provides a lower cost structure for conducting business. Agencies are going to be forced to do business on that basis more and more, but should never lose sight of the importance of making global messages culturally relevant at the local level.

Getting Messages Across in Countries Whose Technology Varies From Ours

Technology leapfrogs. It doesn't progress on a predictable straight line. Cell phone and wireless technology developed relatively more quickly in Latin America than in the U.S. because the landline infrastructure of the national telecommunications companies was so unreliable; cell phone usage just exploded. This illustrates the importance of having local media specialists who thoroughly understand the local business environment. Technology is going to develop in different ways at different rates in different countries, and that will fundamentally change the way we communicate with consumers. As an industry we need to be highly flexible and adaptable and ready to maximize new technologies whenever and wherever they become available.

Reinventing Brands Versus Remaining Consistent

A brand needs to stay relevant. Sometimes that involves less reinvention and is more a challenge of creatively communicating why the brand continues to have meaning for people. We strive to tap a brand's universal truth to motivate and inspire, one that is derived from the core essence of the brand.

Measure ROI With Respect to Advertising

You have to introduce different messages to different consumer groups and understand the messages you put in front of each. You then relate those messages back to the desired change in behavior. Today, because of the way media has fragmented and the response measurement tools that are available, we can be far smarter about how we put that message into the marketplace and how we measure its effectiveness. Marketers and their agencies need to aggressively pursue different options in real time, and then quickly act on those response rates that are driving better business results and replicate them across broad geographies very quickly. There are already tools out there that will correlate business results to communications and marketing activity in real time, and they will only become more sophisticated.

Major Pitfalls to Avoid in Advertising

The biggest pitfalls are not clearly defining objectives, and not pushing for the breakthrough while accepting the ordinary. A number of clients today are marketing for incremental gain instead of disruptive change. The smartest marketers are willing to break through barriers. They're not looking for a 3-5% sales gain; they're looking for something that's going to rewrite the rules of the marketplace and create a new set of rules that everyone wants to follow.

Becoming a Leader in the Advertising World

Being a real leader in this business takes more guts than imagination. The ad industry is slow to innovate, slow to change. It operates on principles that its founders established in the late 19th century. That's why there's a real opportunity for people who want to run through walls, and whose philosophy is "Get out of my way".

Impressive Characteristics About Other Leaders Within the Advertising Industry

Intelligence impresses me. A combination of people smarts, street smarts and pure smarts - animals that go into a situation and figure out a way to win. I'm impressed by organizations that deliver a universal standard of superior performance as a best practice throughout the enterprise. They do great work across their client base as opposed to a small number of showcase accounts.

Type of People Needed on a Successful Advertising Team

Smart, highly motivated people, who know how to teach and who embrace change with all its pain and disruption. We need good communicators, instinctive salespeople.

The Future of Advertising

Invitation is fundamentally and universally displacing Intrusion. During the economic expansion of the 1990s, a lot of the sins of the industry were papered over with economic growth. The day of reckoning is coming and a number of media companies and agencies that do not have sound business models are going to pass from the scene.

The advertising industry is most lax in understanding how people receive messages and how to create compelling messages. Until recently, our industry has been dominated by the creative function at the exclusion of all else. Creative is essential, but the leading marketing communications companies of the future will have three core competencies:

Fact-driven customer knowledge at the individual level derived from sophisticated database management tools;

Superior media capabilities that allow us to effectively make contact and interact with our target consumer across a variety of media disciplines;

Innovative creative ideas, flawlessly executed, that inspire and motivate consumers to invite the brand into their lives - with absolutely no regrets.

In 2001, Bob Brennan assumed the role of president, Leo Burnett Worldwide, with geographic responsibility for North America, senior management responsibilities on several key multinational clients and the task of driving key strategic initiatives globally. His move to Leo Burnett demonstrates Bcom3's determination to alter the way 'traditional' agencies operate.

Since Leo Burnett launched Starcom as a separate media operation in 1997, Bob Brennan has evolved with the company as it proved itself a key player in the media arena, emerged as a worldwide force, and now exists as Starcom MediaVest Group, a top five global media organization. As chief operating officer of SMG, Bob helped the company achieve an unmatched level of prominence in the industry, as well as win several billion dollars of new business, including the unprecedented $2.9 billion media planning AOR for General Motors.

Bob joined Burnett in 1982 as a media buyer/planner. By 1986, he was an assistant media director and was elected a vice president in 1988. The following year, he was named media director, ultimately overseeing McDonald's global media account. He was then elected a senior vice president in 1994. Beginning in 1995, Bob spent two years benchmarking competitors and uncovering the best practices of leading media operations around the world as director of international media. This experience prompted enhancements to Starcom's advanced systems and media research tools, including the drive to bring optimization systems to the U.S.

.

ACHIEVING SUCCESS
AS A TEAM

David Bell
Interpublic Group
Vice Chairman

Exciting Aspects of the Advertising Industry

What is paradoxically most exciting about today's ad industry is that it now extends well beyond traditional advertising. It remains at its core a close ally of corporate marketing and CEOs in driving revenue, but has broadened out to interconnect with all of the tools of communication to accomplish this goal. No longer are ad campaigns the primary concern of marketing groups and CEO's. They often provide the centerpiece, but other disciplines may also be at the center of the effort or surround the advertising in seeking to drive revenue and gain share. But the essence of what an advertising team has to do has remained unchanged - except that it needs to operate in concert with the other disciplines to be able to deliver complete solutions.

Services That Ad Agencies Should Provide

The traditional services - which are certainly the core of any great advertising agency - are the disciplines of strategic planning, creation, media, and marketing consultation. Having these basic disciplines operate as a team to deliver an advertising solution is critical. However, in one way or another, the great agencies have all transformed themselves to reflect a much broader offering, although they've done it through different models. This broader offering encompasses a capability for one to one communication through direct marketing, and also in digital forms. It also includes transactional promotion disciplines that are important in any marketing mix. And it often includes consulting, research, sports marketing, event marketing, speakers - all of the tools that major holding companies have in their arsenals today.

Goal for an Advertising Campaign

The goal of an advertising campaign is to cement a unique bond between the advertiser and consumer. It should simultaneously touch on an emotional and rational need on the part of the consumer and link that need to what the advertiser is offering. Different agencies have varying philosophies on the role of advertising, but the goal is ultimately to provide a bond. Another underlying belief is that a great commercial or ad always has to have an idea. Without an idea, it is very difficult to get into that emotional segment of a consumer's being. An idea must have enduring value and be campaignable. It must stand the test of time. Advertising is far better if it is sustainable so that you are building on it and creating a relationship rather than simply having a single albeit positive impression. Lastly, I believe that there must be an element of surprise - it is far better for somebody to notice an ad once than to ignore it three or four times.

Changes in the Industry

Our business is defined by change. Clearly, the digital revolution has made far more one-on-one forms of communication possible. And I think the new technology of the digital revolution has added opportunities to the traditional ad campaign. Certainly the different kinds of products that are advertised have also placed new demands on advertising. For example, the direct-to-consumer advertising from pharmaceutical manufacturers is designed to help provide consumers with information that allows them to pursue personalized health care. In the United States, the growing trend towards multiculturalism has added a dimension that is important for advertisers and marketers as well.

Importance of Branding

I think branding is a great definition of the bond between a company and the consumer. There has been testimony in Washington that a brand is really a trust mark. It embodies characteristics that make their customers' lives easier by allowing them to make informed choices between a myriad of options. Advertising is but one place where a brand touches a consumer. The touch points have become numerous, cross-disciplinary, and must be managed well if a brand is to stand for something and if a brand is to have strength in the enormous clutter that exists. Managing the multiple branding points is enormously important. That's where today's integration begins.

Integrated Marketing

The notion of "integrated marketing" as a set of words is a bit bankrupt. In effect, it was a spectacular failure as a product launch. It failed because it violated one of the principles of product launch. It lacked the "what's in it for me" concept, the "me" being the target audience - the advertisers. The "what's in it for me" was only clear-cut for the agencies from its inception: integrated marketing was meant to sell additional services. This push came in the wake of most of the agencies having already bought or added these services. As a result, what should have been - and still is - at its core a great concept, failed. In large part it failed because most advertisers weren't organized to deal with it. There were huge silos involved in many of the marketing organizations, sales promotion departments with their budgets, direct-marketing markets with their budgets and so on. Inside the company there was rarely any call for integration.

As advertisers have downsized and streamlined by taking costs out of their organization, they have come to the point where the marketing decisions tend to be far more centralized and tied to the top. Today what's increasingly called for is an overall look at the total marketing budget and then determining the most efficient way of distributing it and making it work.

Favorite Communications Tools

One of my favorite tools has become public relations. A third party writing about a campaign or an issue contained in a campaign can turbo charge the efficacy of the work, and can broaden its credibility and scope dramatically.

Online/Interactive Advertising

I definitely believe that online advertising is going to grow. The question is what forms Internet advertising will take, as it's in the early stage of evolution. The banner-based Internet advertising economy is morphing into a new form of advertising utilizing the Web in tandem with other content providers. I think it will be interesting to watch how the Internet advertising economy moves from being a stand-alone kind of business to one that integrates better with other communications.

Importance of Creativity and Innovation

Unfortunately creativity is a difficult word to define. You will not find an advertising agency on the planet that would not argue that creativity is their number one focus. It is hard to measure what is creative. However, if you spend any time in our industry, it becomes easy to recognize creativity. Real creativity, though, is extraordinarily difficult. It involves risk, and does not respond well to timetables. The creative magic that comes from the minds of people who use their associative intelligence in new ways happens in an environment where they are appreciated, accepted, and respected. This happens when clients appreciate the magic that creativity can bring to a static strategy or to a marketing program.

Best Ways to Calculate ROI on a Campaign

The current state of the art in our industry is rapidly evolving. As always in our industry there are many claims to having "cracked the code". I think that serious students could raise issues with the veracity of some of these models. The point is that the situation is evolving rapidly, and the focus is definitely on cross-platform ROI issues. It is my belief that in the next decade, we will see giant advances in the proprietary tools for measuring and assessing ROI on a pre and post facto basis.

Importance of Environment

I absolutely believe that the best work and best solutions come out of an environment where there is mutual respect and trust. The little secret of our business is that any advertiser can get a disproportionate share of the best minds in our business simply by creating the right environment. People in our business have choices, and if there is an excitement among creative people to come to work on a project where they know that an environment is positive, they tend to gravitate towards it. Environment can trump nearly everything.

Major Pitfalls to Avoid

Boredom. The lack of risk taking. The unwillingness to push the envelope. The biggest risk in advertising is doing good work because it keeps you from doing great work. It allows you to be complacent, to coast along without pushing, and without rejecting. You have to be willing to let the magical spark of creativity occur beyond the obvious.

Killer Applications That Will Revolutionize Advertising

I think the killer apps that will revolutionize the advertising world in the next decade will come from serious marketing applications of databases and database techniques. I also believe that the advent of experiential media and pervasive media using the wireless platform will have a large impact on our business. The desire to stand out continues to push the industry forward. I have on my desk a new technique that allows advertisers to create three-dimensional building advertising, which is absolutely stunning. As an adjunct to other branding pieces, it is incredible.

Globalization and Consolidation

I think the twin trends of globalization and consolidation are going to continue. It is important to recognize that the consolidation trend among advertising companies was really started by the consolidation trend among clients. We have responded aggressively and dramatically. Globalization is a companion trend that will continue to occur because clients look for both the efficiencies and the single branding issues, recognizing that large segments of our population today are truly global consumers as opposed to regional consumers.

Becoming a Leader in the Industry

I think for an individual to be a leader in this business, you have to love the creative process. To start, you really have to believe that working with other people to generate ideas that can make a difference is the ultimate challenge. Advertising practitioners tend to have a number of characteristics in common, and I have spent time talking to human resources about what they tend to be. One personal characteristic is optimism, which is normally the hallmark of most successful advertisers simply because they are entering a world of rejection of creative work and hiring. There is volatility in the business that is undeniable. Innate optimism is a necessary ingredient. A second aspect is being aggressive. I would say that passivity is not the hallmark of leaders. Then third, visual acuity is needed. I would also say that a certain emotionalism and passion as a thread through the first three is also essential. The last key to success in the business is the ability to team effectively. You need an ability to work in teams, and quickly form new ones, to find the way to bring people together and make things happen. Creation is both a team sport and a solo sport, but the bulk of our business relies on effective teams to make things happen. The reality is that a well-oiled team of above-average skill will beat a team that is highly skilled but ragged nearly every day (by "ragged" I mean filled with politics and unnecessary individualism).

Effective Management Styles

There are a couple of effective management styles in our business, although I don't necessarily believe they are styles as much as differing emphases among shared attributes. First, a successful leader is always able to clearly and crisply articulate the priorities. The second is that a leader needs to be able to translate those priorities in ways that connect with the people who are going to execute them. The other thing that tends to characterize leaders in our business is that they are focused on growing their clients' business.

Long term, if a client is not growing their business on some dimension in conjunction with their relationship with the partner, the relationship is going to fail.

Admirable Aspects of Other Advertisers

What impresses me about certain leaders is the intensity of their focus, seriousness of purpose, and their willingness not to take themselves too seriously. What impresses me most about advertisers are those who can set the bar high and have clear expectations. Those who are decisive, who can articulate what they want and create an environment where people want to jump through walls on their behalf because they know they will be appreciated and respected for doing that.

Successful Advertising Team

I think you have to start with a group of people that can leave their own egos behind in favor of a team objective. Then you have to have a team that wants to break new ground all the time and swing for the fences on everything they do. They have to resist the temptation simply to be good. There needs to be skill in each position, and those skill sets tend to be different. For example, a brilliant strategic planner can come from lots of different disciplines, but will always be consumer-focused. The greatest strategic planners are people who truly love observing other people and understanding them by trying to penetrate why people react, think, and feel the way they do. That skill is essential to the advertising creation team. Of course, the other disciplines have their own unique strengths as well.

Staying on Top of the Industry

The best advice that I ever had on staying on top of the industry came from a serious member of the creative community who said that advertising people keep their edge by reading everything. Not just about the advertising business, but everything. It may come from strange places. During the Internet economy it might have come from Red Herring and Fast Company. It might come from the New England Journal of Medicine or National Geographic. Ultimately, it comes from gathering seemingly unrelated information and spotting trends that are occurring in the minds of consumers and understanding what they are feeling and thinking. In addition to doing the obvious homework one would do in any industry, getting out ahead requires absorption of all kinds of other things that may or may not seem to be relevant at the moment. Hollywood, the music business, intellectual thought, cutting edge kinds of publications, new venues - all of those have an impact on the work that we do in being able to create the advertising bond with consumers.

The Future of the Advertising World

I think the trick will be to marry the digitally based and data-driven information with the hugely right brain creative activity that has proven its strength not only in advertising but also across all the disciplines we touch. The most exciting part will be how we use more new empirical information combined with the magic of creation to produce solutions that we'd never have imagined.

David Bell is one of the advertising and marketing communications industry's foremost leaders. He was recently named Vice Chairman of The Interpublic Group of Companies, the world's largest marketing communications and services company. He also serves on Interpublic's Board of Directors.

Until its recent merger with Interpublic, Mr. Bell was Chairman and Chief Executive Officer of True North Communications Inc., the world's ninth largest global advertising and marketing communications holding company. Under his leadership, True North realigned and strengthened its agency brands, including FCB Worldwide, BSMG and Marketing Drive, and expanded the company's global competitiveness - while significantly improving its financial performance. He also established a culture of collaboration across True North brands on behalf of clients seeking broader solutions, significantly driving organic growth.

Before becoming CEO of True North in April, 1999, Mr. Bell had been President and Chief Executive Officer of Bozell Worldwide, a leading advertising agency. Earlier, he served as President of Bozell's Atlantic and Midwest divisions. He came to Bozell in 1975, when the agency acquired Knox Reeves Advertising, where he had been President since 1972. Prior to that, he was an Executive Vice President; the agency's youngest Vice President; and an Account Executive. He began his career at Leo Burnett in its Executive Development Program.

THINK LIKE THE SUN: THE SECRET TO BUILDING GLOBAL LOVEMARK BRANDS

TIM LOVE

Saatchi & Saatchi

Managing Partner

Exciting Aspects of Advertising: Ideas

I get really excited when I believe I have an idea and I think that it can motivate and address issues or needs that people have which can help change their lives. This can be a cause-related societal need or a physical or emotional need. The excitement that I get when I have an idea or strategy that can help motivate people and change events is really exciting. When you have an idea you really want to see if it works. It just takes over. I think this is true of a lot of people in the advertising business. They are very much motivated by the power of ideas and the recognition from seeing their ideas have an impact on people's lives. It's why people say advertising is more art than science. It's not just art, but it's not just science either. This business has a lot to do with the creative feeling and inspiration you get by helping people and helping brands be successful and relevant. The planning that goes into developing a campaign is exciting, because of the anticipation, discipline, setting it up and, then, creating it. The day you start to see whether or not it has an effect is tremendously exciting.

Importance of Brands in Today's Society

There is an evolution in brands that is going on. The first stage of brand evolution was from product to trademark, when the manufacturer of the product decided they wanted to protect that product for legal reasons. They trademarked their products. As competition came in for that product or service, the concept of branding started. Branding was a way to leverage a point of difference within competing products or services.

The next stage of evolution happened from 1970-1990, and the impetus was consumerism. Consumerism was the time when we started to realize that our consumers wanted more information on the impact the product could have on them in the broader context of their usage of the service or brand. This is the time when we started to see brands put more information on packaging, and put more information at the disposal of the consumer about how the product was made, it's health impact, caloric content, where it was made, environmental impact and contents, etc. We believe that phase of brand development was really where brands evolved into "Trustmarks", because in order to maintain loyalty and to seek appeal from consumers for a brand or service, the consumer wanted more information. If you didn't give adequate performance on your promises or if you did not give sufficient information, you didn't achieve trust.

What has happened more recently with the rapid pace of change that we've seen at the end of the Cold War and the proliferation of media globally, as well as the penetration of new media such as the Internet, has given the customer the ability to seek more information about brands. We believe that brands are evolving into a need to have a "Lovemark" relationship with consumers. It's what our company is coining as a nomenclature to get people to understand that the consumers are looking for a far more in-depth relationship with the brands and the services that they devote their loyalty too.

Lovemarks

It used to be that brand effort was to primarily gain a transaction - a purchase or subscription of service. Today's marketing environment is a Global Village. In this new global village there is so much information that there is a need to move to a more emotional appeal and connection between brands and consumers in order to achieve loyalty. The first point is that brands and consumers are moving from a time of transactions to relationships. We are not afraid to think about or talk about it as a long lasting love affair. What goes into establishing a long lasting love affair is a very emotional, caring, attentive and one-to-one relationship with information flowing back and forth.

Lovemarks were first discussed by Kevin Robert's, our CEO last October in 'Fast Company' magazine. He was asked a question about brands and evolution. What we have spent a lot of time and effort on is to globally study the aspects of brands, leadership, loyalty, and the relationship people have with their brands. Consumers will increasingly seek a Lovemark relationship with their brands that will allow them to have a greater one-to-one dialogue. The reason is that the media now allows them to have a greater dialogue with brands and companies than ever before. You can use the Internet or the telephone to find out a lot of information about your brand, who makes it, where it is made, and what is in it. It is moving beyond the rational sale or connection that consumers used to have with their brands. Having good or acceptable product performance is still key to success. However, having good performance is table stakes. To achieve loyalty in markets where product performance differences are not sustainable for a long time, you need an emotional connection to sustain your brand.

This is why a lot of researchers are saying that we are evolving to a time of great customization of brands and services. We are working to become much more customized to consumer needs. For our clients and our brands, we have people available to talk to them twenty-four hours a day. If consumers have information questions, they can go to the website. If a consumer can't talk to somebody, your brand is not going to have a relationship for very long. Just like a long lasting love affair, if you stop communicating, the relationship withers.

Lovemarks Transcend Mere Brands

Lovemarks reach not only into consumers' hearts and minds but into their very lives. Take a brand away and people will find a replacement. Take a Lovemark away and people will protest its absence. Because people never merely buy Lovemarks, they embrace them. Passionately. And never let go. Let's take a look at some examples.

We think that an example of a Lovemark, (there aren't that many that exist yet globally), is a company like Disney. You think about Disney in your life and how they continue to be an amazing brand, with an experience that is always fresh, engaging, relevant and emotional. Another one is Harley Davidson. Some of these brands lose their way, but they tend to recapture the essence of the love that people had for them. Harley Davidson is a great case history with the resurrection of the brand, the sound of the engine, and the look of it. The mystique has been expanded into all kinds of things like apparel. It all happened when Harley Davidson improved their product performance and began the leveraging of their beloved symbols and equities.

Another example is Tide. It has an incredible relationship with consumers over the years and it continues to be vital and growing today because Tide is creating a more emotional relationship and connection with its consumers. If you think about all the detergents out there and all the new ones that come and go, Tide continues to be such a solid brand because of the Lovemark relationship it has with it's users. Having a Lovemark relationship, like a love affair, cannot be taken for granted. We think that brands reside in people's homes, while a Lovemark resides in their heart. Brands are about information, but a Lovemark is about a relationship. A Lovemark is like a great lover - it is always seducing, but never gets boring.

Another emerging Lovemark is Toyota. There was a report earlier this year about car sales in the United States in which Detroit car sales were down between 15-18%. However, during the same period, Toyota sales were up 6.7%. When people have a Lovemark relationship for a brand, they start to rely on that brand in times of need and devote more of their time and loyalty to that brand.

Apple is another great example of a brand with Lovemark stature. Americans loved Apple in the early 80's. Apple lost their way a little bit, but the next thing you know they are coming out with the iMac, which has great colors and transparent panels showing the tubes in the back of the computer. The design and emotional attitude of the new iMac were fantastically received by consumers.

Another example of a Lovemark is the VW Beetle. They lost their way, and weren't meeting the acceptable level of rational product performance for quite some time. When they brought back the Beetle design and in such interesting new colors, a love affair was waiting to be rekindled. People have a funny relationship with their Beetles. They want to touch them and be close to them all the time. This couldn't have happened, if they hadn't restored an acceptable level of performance as table stakes on the rational part of the sale that is so important.

Another Lovemark is Tylenol. They had a horrible thing happen with the tampering incident. This was something that could have easily killed any other brand. However, people love Tylenol, and they wanted Tylenol to do something about the problem, while they didn't blame them. When Tylenol took decisive action and removed the capsule product and moved to the hard caplet, this was seen as a very responsible thing by the people who have a love affair with Tylenol. Now Tylenol continues to have that kind of Lovemark relationship with their consumers.

Basically what consumers are expecting of any brand is that the rational performance aspects have to be met.

Moving to try and build an emotional relationship requires that you deliver on the expected, acceptable level of product performance that consumers are looking for. We call that the "table stakes". If you don't provide an acceptable level of rational product or service performance, you are never going to be able survive in this new world of so many brand choices and messages bombarding people. It is a world where competition can match your performance more quickly from other parts of the planet.

Exciting Things on the Forefront of the Industry

Globalization. While everyone knows that globalization is going on and there is a lot debate about currency and the ability to ship goods back and forth between countries, there is a major restructuring going on as we start to actually see what Marshall McLuhan said would happen - the "Global Village". It doesn't mean that people are all becoming the same, but it does mean that they have access to information about brands more than ever and from anywhere on the planet.

Many professionals in marketing and advertising have adopted the perspective of "Think Global, Act Local". I believe it is time to retire that phrase and concept. I believe this was a useful concept in the early stages of globalization, around the end of the Cold War, and the tearing down of the Berlin Wall. This was the time when we started seeing a major reconstruction of business in Europe and an opening to greater trade relationships with countries like China. The notion of "Think Global, Act Local" was a message to people that there were other markets out there, besides the ones they were living and dealing with in their own country. It made people realize the importance of thinking about markets outside your geography. However, it was inherently a geographic concept that did not provide an ideal perspective for the brand building that started to happen and continues to happen as the media explodes and creates a smaller and smaller world – the global village.

The effect that media growth is having on the way business is conducted is tremendous. You can see it in our own media consumption in the U.S. I can say from traveling all over the world, that I could sit in Europe and be able to watch sumo wrestling if I got to the right satellite channel.

There is stuff coming in from all over the world, and this is having the same kind of effect on our global society and environment as radio first had in the United States when it brought news and imagery of something outside your own village into your kitchen.

The first truly, global brand was Y2K. I know that may be surprising to a lot of people but think about what Y2K was. You remember anticipation building up to it, all the concern and warnings that the earth was going to have problems and that electricity would go off, that there would be severe outages and shortages of food that it would be a harbinger of bad times between people. Then, when the day happened, Y2K came; the whole world saw something occur as it unfolded around the planet. A sense of well-being and joy and fun swelled for those of us who watched it on television.

It was something that everybody remembers as Y2K. It was the first truly global brand, the first truly global brand experience. I remember the day; I remember getting up that New Year's morning. My kids were in the next room watching television as I was working on something. I recall hearing the news coverage from Wellington in New

Zealand and how they were having a party and everything was fine. There was videotape of the night before and how the New Year's celebration was just fine, none of the computers went out, there were no shortages, there were no killings, there were no demonstrations and riots. It was one great big party. Then, the television news traveled to Sydney where they also had a great celebration going on. It was wonderful to see, they were just celebrating. So Y2K had already been born in those geographies and everything was fine.

Then they cut to Tiannemen Square, a place where there have been many significant news events. In Tiannemen, the Chinese were having a great celebration of good will and harmony for the people of the world. And, as that day unfolded and the coverage of the New Year's Day celebrations and Y2K events around the world going from China to India to Eastern Europe to Russia to London to Paris and to New York to Vancouver, things where just wonderful. We all came away with such a positive feeling about what Y2K was. In that respect it is a brand, it's probably the most well known brand, a brand in which people have a commonly good feeling and experience about. What was an interesting thing to me is how the perception prior to the event and after was so different.

As I go about looking at helping my clients with global communications objectives, as well as local communications and marketing challenges, I believe a new marketing perspective is needed. As I said earlier, I think it's time to retire the idea of "Think Global and Act Local". It made us realize we can't be blind to what's happening in the marketplace or with competition outside of the geography in which we are dealing with. So I think "Think Global and Act Local" was tremendously helpful, initially. However it does not reflect the acceleration in media convergence and information we've seen over the last 5 years.

I believe we need a new perspective and I call this new perspective "Think Like The Sun". When we think about our brands, our businesses and competition we need to "Think Like The Sun".

When we get up in the morning the sun comes up and we go to work and we work on our brands, or businesses. We work all day long to care, nurture, create, get ideas and seek information to help grow our brands and businesses. At the end of the day, when the sun goes down, we turn the lights off and we go home. It is easy to think that our brand and our business kind of stops, in a way, for that evening. We go home, put our head on our pillow and we fall asleep. For all intents and purposes, our brand or business seems to stop in suspension until the next day and the new dawn when the sun comes up. We then resume our activities to drive that brand to success. That's the way it seems.

You know that's not what happens. The sun doesn't go up and down, it's we here on earth that revolve. The sun remains constant and we at our place on the planet are revolving and turning.

Increasingly, with an interconnected media environment, that's fully-wired, proliferating worldwide television and Internet technology we are no longer operating in isolation, our world is a "global village" and this global village is increasingly connected to each other. So, our brands and our businesses are making contact with consumers outside the realm of what we see, beyond the day and the night, as we market our brand in our own geography. Like the sun, our brands and business are making contact with consumers, somewhere, all the time.

The Changing Landscape of Advertising

Regardless of what profession you are in, we all like to tell people about how much more complicated and scientific it is today than compared to what it once was, whether you are a construction engineer, a journalist, or an advertiser. I believe advertising is much more scientific today because of the tools we have at our disposal. There is a greater arsenal of media and tools in which I can try to communicate with somebody.

We call this media evolution the "Age of Also". When the radio first came out and started to be used, people thought newspapers would die, but they didn't. When the television began to be used by people, some people predicted that the radio would die, but it didn't. When CNN first came out, they predicted magazines would go away, but there are more magazines today than there have ever been. With the Internet, they predicted television would diminish, but it hasn't. It is just more complicated and there is a greater breadth of media being consumed by people. This is why we call it the "Age of Also", when it comes to media.

Every time a new media comes in during the "Age of Also" it is in addition to all the other media. There are only twenty-four hours a day though. I heard a talk given by Bob Pittman of AOL. He said that the Internet is "convenience in a box". He was talking about the increased penetration levels the Internet is receiving, something we read about every day. Now with the collision of Internet, broadband, and television, it is going even further.

With only twenty-four hours in the day, what are people doing? The first two activities being replaced by greater consumption of media are sleep and eating. People tend to be sleeping less and spending less time eating. You know where you might see that effect - look at the fast food consumption and the decline in families sitting down for breakfast and dinner. People are moving to handheld portable foods, where they can eat with one hand and use a device in another. Cup holders in cars and multi-tasking are really interesting, and this is what is happening in the Age of Also. Again this is why consumers in this time-starved world of intense information are looking for brand relationships that are truly relationships, not just a transaction.

The other part about the industry is as simple as having a relationship with somebody. It is about caring, being considerate, listening, asking what their needs are, and anticipating their needs. That is the essence of the advertising industry. It always has been and always will be. In the 1920's, Claude Hopkins wrote a book about the advertising industry called *Scientific Salesmanship*. He was the highest paid copywriter at the time, he was paid more than the President of the United States or Babe Ruth. A bunch of journalists went to talk to him and asked him how he came up with his great ideas. He was sitting in his office in Chicago and said that his solution was that he always did something he call "The Hat Trick". They all scribbled down what he was saying, and then asked him what a "Hat Trick" was. He said that he would get out of his office, take the hat off of his hat rack, and go out and stand in a store watching consumers. Then, he would talk to them and find out what they wanted. Sam Walton, the founder of Wal-Mart, also had a great saying. He said that he "had the secret" - all you have to do is "listen to the consumer and give them what they want". This is the simple part that sometimes gets overshadowed by the new tools and complexity that we use in the scientific part of a business. This is why it is a business of both science and art. There is no question that the science is becoming more scientific, but there is also no question that the art of it is as simple and beautiful as it always has been. It has to do with building a relationship with somebody. I believe science costs money, whereas art costs passion. This is why I believe our Lovemarks way of thinking about brand relationships is so right for today. It recognizes the value of passion in the art of building brand relationships.

Killer Applications That Affect Industry

One of the things I really believe in is something that was said by a famous historian named Hegal in the 1800's. He said, "What we learn from history is that we don't learn from history". Harry Truman and George Bernard Shawn also said this.

I look at the effect that television and radio have had. I think changes in media have a profound effect on society, business, and the way that people relate to each other.

Marshall McLuhan studied the effect of media from the time of hieroglyphics to the Guttenberg press and on to the electronic media. The press enabled people to codify, transport, rewrite, and communicate history. It was amazing what it did. The Bible is a good off shoot of that. Consider the telephone and the effect that media had on enabling people to talk with people outside where they were, in the next village or the other side of the country. This brought societies closer together. Think about the television, one of the biggest innovations, because it brought sight, sound, and motion right into your home. It is more sensory than any other media because it incorporated these three senses.

The next big one, and we are at the early stages of this, is the convergence of the high speed Internet and the television. It will combine our ability to communicate one-to-one with the most sensory media of all time, television. Broadband is the next leapfrog for this consolidation between the Internet and television. If you think about it, Internet is related to the telephone, television, wireless, and radio. Broadband is going to help consolidate all of this, to give people greater access to information by putting the power in the hands of the consumer of the information as opposed to the giver of the information. That is the biggest and most exciting thing that this new application is going to give us, and it is already changing the way we talk to people and the amount of information we give them in our business. It is changing the relationships we seek to have with them.

Key Requirement to Becoming a Leader

Integrity. I think this because everything is so much more transparent in this global village. It is true both for our brands and for us as individuals who come up with ideas. The truthfulness and integrity about full disclosure of what your brand's real essence is, its reason for being, and why someone should choose you. The root of that is integrity, just like in a relationship. There is going to be a tape player somewhere, a phone mail message, or Internet connection somewhere. If you want to find out about anyone - Tim Love, where he went to school, whether he is married, what schools his kids attend, basically anything you want to know, you can find out about it. I think having personal integrity is very important. The leaders in the future must have extremely high integrity.

Another reason, is that it is a much more accountable world in business and it will continue to be. Our clients will increasingly want us to be accountable for our suggestions, advice, and the work that we propose to them for their brands and services. Does it work? Does it have a positive effect on the business? As a result, we are seeing changes in the compensation structures, we are moving away from a simple formula of commission on paid media to a fee-based compensation. More compensation is tied to delivery of results. What underlies all of this is integrity and the desire that people become more accountable to each other.

Admirable Aspects of Other Advertisers

Number one, I am most impressed by advertisers and leaders who are willing to do the right thing, even though it might not seem like the conventional or expedient thing to do. To do the right thing when it might not have a positive short-term impact on their business or themselves personally is very admirable. Two business leaders who I admire most are John Pepper and AG Lafley, the Chairman and CEO at Procter and Gamble respectively. They both have high integrity. The leaders I admire most exhibit high integrity in their professional approach to the business they do. That same integrity is apparent in their contribution of involvement and helping improve the lives of people beyond the business they have. I admire people in my industry who take their skill and expertise and try to apply it to cause related activity that can help improve the lives of people.

Saatchi & Saatchi has a remarkable history of being involved in cause related efforts that we don't get paid for, or we do because we care. We have a lot of individuals giving their time and talents to help many activities on a pro bono basis. This past June, a 30-year retrospective of this creative work was put on exhibit in our offices. We were honored that The Heart of America Foundation in Washington DC, a not-for-profit organization and Mr. Christopher Reeve, the actor and activist, came to give us an award for Corporate Responsibility. I am really proud of that. That makes me feel good about the integrity of what we are doing.

John Pepper gave a speech called the "Boa Principle". He used the analog of a boa constrictor to doing the right thing. He said that all of us in our lives are daily confronted with value judgments that we have to make. Some of these seem almost invisible to us because that's our job. What he said was that you really can't separate the two in terms of your personal integrity. These things operate much like a boa constrictor. People think a boa constrictor just wraps itself around you and squeezes until you suffocate. That's not how it works. A boa wraps itself around your chest cavity and stays put. It is sensitive to when you breathe out. When you breath out it constricts each time. Gradually, it reaches a point where you can't breathe in any more. That's the boa principle.

I admire leaders who demonstrate that they are operating their business and their lives with a high degree of social consciousness. I happen to think that is going to be an increasingly important thing in this new world where there is greater accessibility of information, dialogue and transparency.

A Successful Advertising Team

I like to be around people who have insatiable curiosity. I believe what is required from a team is an inherent belief that "nothing is impossible". In some ways, I was going to say rebelliousness, but this doesn't capture it. It is the willingness to challenge conventional wisdom and to seek the impossible. This starts by believing in your heart that nothing is impossible. It's a passionate and restless belief in this. If you don't have a team around you that believes this, it is really hard to move the needle from point A to point B. If you think about some of the huge challenges we have at large, like trying to counteract the effect of drugs, alcoholism, or misperception about cultures and people's personal beliefs or behaviors, we need to be insatiably curious and optimistic to address these daunting challenges. You have to believe nothing is impossible. I know it is a very idealistic view. However, I've found it is the best attitude for meeting challenges in the advertising and marketing communications business.

The Future of the Advertising World

I believe you will see a continuation of not learning from history. There will also be a continuation of globalization in integrated communications as the "Age of Also" evolves further. We will see more convergence in the media and businesses across geographies. What we will see is an increasing appreciation for diversity and celebration of individuality. It is already happening with the younger generation who are consuming more diverse media over the time. Our kids are much more open to diversity of appearance, lifestyle, and opinion than the previous generation.

The multicultural international sensitivity that will be happening as a result of the media is going to have a tremendous affect on the world of the advertising. It means that, like most businesses, we have to be willing to change and transform ourselves. Everybody talks about the need to change, just look at the past year and a half with the transformation of the dot.com business and the "new economy" versus the "old economy". We need to plan for change. We say here that we are moving from a "knowledge economy", to a "change economy". The future is going to be built on continual plans for anticipated change. We have to build it in and prepare for it, because like that love affair, it gets a little boring if we don't keep things interesting and fresh.

Before joining Saatchi & Saatchi in 1999, Tim was Worldwide Account Director and a member of the Worldwide Board of Directors at D'Arcy Masius Benton & Bowles International (DMB&B). There, in addition to overseeing the global Pillsbury and P&G accounts and winning creative awards for Pampers and Kraft Food's Maxwell House Coffee, he was instrumental in helping P&G globally extend their spectrum of brands, including Pampers, Charmin, Crest, Always, Vick's and Swiffer.

Tim held several senior management positions in DMB&B's New York headquarters from 1989-92 before moving to Brussels, Belgium in late 1992 and assuming overall leadership for that agency's P&G business worldwide. During this time, he led important expansions into Central and Eastern Europe, Africa, the Middle East, Asia and Latin America.

Prior to joining DMB&B, Tim headed his own agency, aptly named Tim Love Advertising. The agency netted billings of $8 million in its first year and created successful national advertising for Lenscrafters, British Knights, Zena Jeans, and the National Committee for Adoption, which won the agency a Bronze Effie for its "Great Expectations" campaign.

SOAK IT ALL IN

PAUL SIMONS

Ogilvy & Mather UK

Chairman & CEO

Exciting Aspects of the Industry

This industry can be incredibly uplifting and exciting. If you pick the things that you get involved in, you can get into things that are genuinely involving. More so today than fifteen years ago, it is easier to create new equities and new brands. Those things are very exciting. Very recently, I went to a launch with a client for a brand we started to create a year ago. I genuinely believe that it will be very big in the UK. We created it from a blank sheet of paper. Those sorts of initiatives are very entrepreneurial but involve a great amount of both analytical thinking to make jumps and creativity to get past the obvious.

Over the past fifteen years, every year I have been heavily involved in doing a launch like that. With my former agency, we launched Sony PlayStation across Europe, and that was an incredibly exciting thing to do. It went from launch to number one in eight months. In the UK, we helped create a new credit card that is now the trendy card to have from nothing in nine months. That is the really exciting thing. If you understand business and really understand where your options lie, advertising in the end is most often the enabler. It is the thing that can take an idea and make it real and live in the public domain.

Greatest Skills

There are two major skills required- creative excellence and business brains. I have always tried to do both things. My training is very much on the analytical side of business - what you are trying to do in the market with the company. I really enjoy that because I am good at it. I can soak up the data, but can get beyond it once I understand it.

The first stage is strategic thinking combined with insight. You need to combine that with an intuitive feel for the creative delivery of that thinking. I am a harsh critic of the creative endeavor because I personally believe if you really push you can end up with something awesome, compelling and persuasive. Too many campaigns end up being ordinary. You tick all the right boxes, but you haven't done anything great. I always push for greatness. Creatives always respond to that immensely well. So it's two things really, it's strategic insight combined with that kind of desire to push the envelope as much as you can.

Challenges Advertisers Face

It is difficult to generalize because almost every sector that you look at has old economy and new economy companies. The challenges they face are very different. That is a caveat to what I am going to say. I believe passionately, and I think the evidence is becoming more obvious, that looking after and growing brands has now become a chief executive's primary job. It can't be left to a functional department like marketing, because their role frequently is helping deliver results. The United States and Europe have demonstrated that the consumer is more willing to try different and new things. Brand owners can't presume that if they are in the top two today, they will be there tomorrow. The huge challenge is how do those companies evolve and sustain their core brand equity in any market? There are so many examples where companies have failed to do that, and have missed it completely. They might be more preoccupied with internal functional things like manufacturing, distribution, or costs. Today more than ever, nobody has a God-given right to remain in a high market position no matter what they do. That is the biggest challenge facing any company, therefore it affects what we do in our industry hugely.

Making an Advertising Campaign Come to Life

The bottom line is that you have to find a way of getting word of mouth. If you can stand in a restroom and hear people talk about a brand or some kind of advertising that you have been involved in, you have succeeded. It tells you much more than what the research says. In our industry, we do a lot of transmitting, but there is not a great deal of receiving because it disappears in that journey. Making something come to life is making it live and breathe where it is received by a lot of people. The test is when it gets talked about, imitated, or lampooned because then you know it has been put in the public domain. If you think about the volume of what is produced, there's a good comparison with the music business. If you think about the number of singles produced every year, only a tiny percentage of what is produced remains in the public's consciousness. The same is true for advertising. Every week there is new stuff going out and probably 95% will be forgotten in a year's time. What I try to do is always be in that memorable 5%. Once it is talked about and remembered it becomes an equity and adds value to a company.

Favorite Mediums of Advertising

I am a bit of traditionalist. I love billboards. I can vividly remember going to Los Angeles and on the journey from the airport to Hollywood, there were all these huge billboards for Nike. The athletes featured were huge cutouts. The power and simplicity of the communication was great. It's one thing to produce all these campaigns through multi-channels of Internet and other things. But you have to stand back for a moment and ask yourself if it really has the power to move people to do something differently. I am a huge fan of propaganda, which is at the heart of what we do. Any medium that can make propaganda work is great. So I am a massive fan of billboards.

In many ways, I am often trying to force people to return to the real basics, to understand what they are trying to do given the plethora of mediums. My starting point is always: If we do this, will it affect enough people to move them? My argument is usually for a propaganda vehicle rather than narrow cast. That's a big debate. The phrase I use a lot is "getting something into public language", which is a very tough thing to do.

The Goal of an Advertising Campaign

This is debated a lot with clients. If I were being Mr. Businessman, I would say return on investment. I think there is a very interesting question here: What is the means and what is the end? If in the end, you are talking about return on the investment made, then you are going to have to interrogate the means. More often than not, the means are not in a logical relationship to the end. If the end is a factual mathematical calculation, it doesn't mean that the means to that end are the same. I think figuring out what the role of advertising is to get you to that end is critical. A lot of companies don't get that right. They attempt to link the two. Many companies will presume you can take the same outcome to drive the means. Often you can't.

If you look at Nike in the UK in the nineties, Nike was very much a niche brand. It was number three or four and only associated with professional athletes, unlike in the United States. It was not a mass brand at all. One of the biggest barriers for Nike to develop across Europe and other parts in the world was its complete absence from soccer. If you are a sporting brand in Europe and you are not in soccer, you have a major problem. How do you get the credentials as a United States brand in terms of soccer? Any company doing marketing by numbers would have said that they couldn't do that until they had distribution.

One of the factors across Europe was that no existing brand owned the emotion of soccer. Various brands were associated with it, but no one had the high moral ground of soccer. The emotion is consistent across any country. We then made this sixty-second spot for TV across Europe shot across three countries. Nike had no distribution at the time - they did not have soccer shoes in any of the stores and most companies would not have done that. But if you earn emotions, it drives the brand and sales, and it also says great things about you as a brand. Once the ad had been on the air for three weeks, they had retailers phoning them frantically begging them to send them Nike soccer shoes. The rest is history. It is a true story. The means and the end may not be logical. Separating out how you do it versus what you are trying to accomplish is such an important thing to do. Many companies don't do it.

Innovation and Creativity in a Campaign

You need a client predisposed to wanting real creativity. That's key. You can take a horse to water, but you can't make it drink. Many brilliant ideas die a death on the way there. Whenever I talk to the president of Sony PlayStation, he ends the call with, "OK, Paul, stay tuned". That's a great expression. You tune into a wavelength. There is a great story about Chiat Day with whom I had the great pleasure of working with. You know the Apple campaign of "think different". Again the story there is fantastic. Creatively, Apple had been all over the place for years. Steve Jobs asked Lee Clow (Chiat Day's creative chief) what he should do. Clow walked in with two boards. One said that Apple had become like any other computer company in the world, and that they could not compete on their turf. The other told them to reinvent the origins of Apple. From that arose "think different".

I have seen innovation numerous times. To get that done, you need a client who wants it, a client who has the vision to understand that they've got to get out of the box, and you need a group of people who have the vision themselves to be able to do it. It takes a lot of energy and people wanting the same answer. Even then there are times when that doesn't happen. There is a quote I use by George Bernard Shaw, "Reasonable men tend to adapt themselves to the world, unreasonable men attempt to adapt the world to themselves, progress is in the hands of unreasonable men". That's a fantastic quote. Wherever you see that kind of leap of imagination, the people who are driving it are not reasonable men and are not accepting of the status quo. They are hungry for a different space and way of doing things. That is not marketing by numbers. You need to know that stuff, but once you do you need a bunch of people to join hands. Any organization that is cautious will never do those things. All of those systems are in place for risk-minimization, and not optimization of opportunity. Therefore, finding an organization that has that mentality is key to making those things happen. You need somebody in the company who gets it and will make it work.

Ideal Relationship With Clients

I think for me, what works best is when I get to the point where I believe there is a genuine openness and a mutual respect between the person leading a company and me. On a personal level, we talk on the same language. You are not dealing with jargon, you know what each other wants to do. When you win the confidence of that person, you can explore what makes sense in terms of what they want to do. That is at the heart of a great relationship. Honesty is very important. Not being afraid to say what you think is very important. Trying to cultivate a culture of open-mindedness is crucially important. They are hard things to do. One of the things I am often asked to talk about is the gap between intent and delivery. What I say is that it is an obstacle race. Everyone has the same intent, but most people never get to the same end. The reason for that is because from the beginning to the end, there are all these obstacles. Most people fall at the second, third, and forth fence. There aren't that many that get to the end of the course. The best relationship one can have is with someone senior that can make things happen, and sidestep the conventional wisdom and prejudice.

What Clients Should Look for in Advertising Agencies

It is a kind of smell. Do you really believe the people you are talking to? Are they talking from their hearts rather than from just a presentation? People who are passionate are very important. You also need talent. Working that out isn't necessarily easy. The clients should really look for the value that the advertising agency can add. We are all good at the basics. We all know how to make advertising, but you want to look at people who can add value to your business. I would take for granted that the top twenty advertising agencies in the United States are proficient in their core skills. For me the question is what they add. This is something that I go to great pains to explain to people. If a client is going to hire somebody, just hiring him or her for the routine stuff is crazy. It's what else that you get that makes a difference in the business.

Killer Applications that Could Revolutionize the Industry

None of us know the answer there, but I think that the big one is going to be interactive television. The jury is out whether or not it is going to work. If it does work, it will make a huge difference to our industry, because it demands different skills. That's one thing. It is certainly lurking in Europe. In the UK it is a reality, because of our own television system, getting interactive television to 50% of our population is easy. In the United States it is harder. That's one big thing. It's true in Europe and Asia as well. That is one big area that is unknown where people are just messing around with it at the moment. We launched the first interactive television station in Britain two years ago. It's amazing how quickly clients started putting money into it because they regard it as another channel of distribution just like the Internet. It's on a medium that is far more familiar to the average person.

The cross over between broadcast television and response medium whether it is interactive TV or the Internet is another big area. The sophistication of CRM, because of software, is something now that can link the two. We are playing with this stuff all the time. It changes what you do, because the effect is more instant. It's not about direct response necessarily, it's more about a seamless line between a broadcast image all the way to consideration. Linking those two is becoming very important. With all that stuff, we all know the linkage between the broadcast spot on TV is important. We know it can happen. Those are the things we are all thinking about.

Differences in the International Landscape

There is a huge drive to globalization of brand equity. Sometimes it is misplaced. It is definitely a truism. There are a number of organizations that are trying to become a Marlboro or a Coke. That is a big issue for many companies. The logic of it is obvious, but whether or not it can be done is another issue. In certain categories, the relevance of the brand is variable by country. The cultural differences do not go away, no matter what anyone says. If you go into the middle of Europe, the cultural differences country by country are so huge. The United States can't be imperialistic about the way it considers its equity globally. It's a big mistake that many Americans are making because they presume the model that works in the United States will work anywhere else, and often it doesn't. Those issues have been around forever, and certainly are not going away.

There is growing consistency for other reasons. For example, rather than looking at product performance, attitude is something that is becoming more consistent globally. Nike is a great example of that. They have a brand built on attitude and are consistent through the world since it cuts through culture differences. There are more and

146

more companies that have cracked a way of positioning their brand that is somehow removed from culture, and has to do with the commonality of attitude. The obvious examples are things based in youth culture. Many of those things are common. You go to a country, and everyone is wearing trainers, and music is similar. Music becomes a great vehicle for advertising because you get borrowed common values. It can cut through cultural differences, because a piece of music that is a hit throughout the world can become a vehicle to help you promote something. Movies are also a really helpful global property because they cut through the cultural divide. All of those things are happening. I just think trying to figure out what turns people on in large numbers is not necessarily the logic of a category, it is the attitude or view people have.

The implications of that for many companies are to look at some of their properties in a different light, which people are doing more now. If somebody is going to play globally, they need some asset that works anywhere and is potent globally. We are all learning but those rules are changing over time.

Becoming a Leader

It takes a combination of things. Determination is part of it. Wanting to do it is important. One of my senior people left because she decided that the demands of her job were too great and she wanted to create a balance in her life. The energy and effort needed to become an ultimate success can be too great. Commitment is also important. It's not a nine to five occupation. You have to be genuinely stimulated by things around you all the time. The stimulus can be different whether it is airports or a hotel room in Paris with CNN. A fascination with environment and stimulus is important. There is definitely a mental skill that is very hard to teach anyone. You have to have a mind that is able to mentally rotate and examine every angle of a situation. Finally, you have to have courage in your convictions. Ultimately, that is what sorts the men from the boys. I have fought passionately for some things in the past even when I have research telling me I am wrong. I don't care what the research says, they are wrong and I am right. I have had people take decisions on the basis of that. You take your life in your hands, but there are times when you think things through and have to say the opportunity is not where the research says. It's all those factors - determination, courage of convictions, dedication, and being mentally agile. I think mental agility is the key to it.

Admirable Aspects of Other Advertisers

The thing I admire most is genuine insight like when someone says they have looked at something and points to the answer, and I say that I wish I had thought of that. I think genuine intellectual insight is a phenomenal quality.

Courage is a quality I admire enormously. Like any creative pursuit, to keep pushing forward requires a huge amount of courage because you have to be prepared to try new sorts of things. Often, with people saying you are wasting money, it takes courage. There is a fabulous book about Bill Bernbach. It is fantastic, fresh, and lovely. There are insights about the VW Beetle and how it is as fresh today as it was when he originally did it. All of his observations about what we do are quite awe-inspiring because there was a man who was very intelligent and creative with a great self-belief. His own beliefs and courage resulted in fabulous work and an incredibly successful advertising agency globally. It's that kind of thing which I admire enormously in other people.

Keeping Your Edge

What I have always done is tried to keep myself at a distance from the day-to-day production of what we do, because most of the people we employ have a short-term vision of what they are doing since there are deadlines. Because of that, I am often able to look at things from a fresh perspective.

Also, I have massive determination always to be pnn the winning team in whatever I do. There are the public endorsements and accolades. Because of that, you can never accept the status quo. For me, it's driven by ego probably. The result of that is always questioning everything that is going on and trying to learn from things. If they are all zigging, why don't we zag? I have a sponge-like mentality. I absorb things very easily, and am very quick to understand stuff. I am very lucky. I go to different parts of the world and see what we are doing, and then I pick out of that stuff that seems to be really innovative or unusual. It is a combination of factors really. The main thing is keeping my head clear of the day-to-day stuff that drags people down.

For our senior people, we are doing executive coaching. It is interesting. The counselor listens to me and analyzes me. She told me that I am kind of unusual because I never ever stop at the latest success. For me, the analogy I have always used is that it is like climbing a mountain. If you ever do climb you can see the horizon and you begin to realize there is another one beyond it. I always look to the next one, therefore you have to figure out how to deal with all the things that get in the way.

Qualities Needed in an Advertising Team

It is pretty straightforward. You have to have balance of disciplines. You need the person that can slough away at the research and summarize it. You need someone who has the ability to constantly make big lateral leaps unfettered by anything else. You have to have a creative talent to listen to everything and suddenly paint a picture. You can't run strategic analysis on television. You have to have that leap.

Having someone in the middle of that who can interpret that stuff is vitally important. I don't think any of those things are surprising because partnerships in our business are critical.

For me there have been many examples where I have partnered the creative so I was the one sitting around trying to figure out what we were going to do. I started with the strategic analysis and worked with the creative person, because the best way to help a creative person is by giving him or her one word or a simple idea. It's always about a team of people who spark off each other.

Sadly, it is a trial and error process. There is no formula that you can use to get the right team, it is a chemical reaction between individuals. I have seen them work fantastically and see them be dismal failures. You can reconfigure the team that is a dismal failure, and they can suddenly become winners because there is something chemical in the relationship between people. It's true, I have seen it at both ends. If you are managing a creative business, you have to be nimble at understanding what works and what doesn't, and then changing the groups of people. It's a business driven by people who are usually optimistic, but it does require leadership and having someone to point to the answer.

The Future of Advertising

The biggest change that is inevitable is a polarization from specialist boutique operations to much larger broad delivery services. There are more and more clients who find the process of managing lots of different specialist operations a royal pain. It soaks up huge amounts of managing time. Most importantly, when large companies are dealing with ten different agencies, something gets lost between the different businesses.

Right now, the challenge for many agency groups is shaking off the historic prejudice that if it is not advertising, it's not worth doing. A lot of agency groups have to carefully rethink the philosophy about what they physically deliver. You have to separate out the big thinking and ideas from implementation. The first thing is the real value. The second bit is something that is great if you can do the whole thing, but from the client's view is not essential. Separating the two halves is becoming a growing trend. It is a very big challenge for many agency groups because many of them are completely dominated by broadcast advertising. That is a very difficult prejudice to break out of it.

Paul Simons is the Chairman and CEO of Ogilvy & Mather UK, one of the country's largest advertising groups. Previously, he was the Chairman of TBWA UK Group, which incorporated seven separate marketing services companies, a staff base of 600 and client relationships in every major sector of industry and commerce.

Simons has a twenty-year advertising background and is best known for his successful advertising campaigns for Sony PlayStation, Nike, Goldfish, The Sun and Virgin, whilst at Simons Palmer, the company he established in 1988.

LIKEABLE ADVERTISING: CREATIVE THAT WORKS

ALAN KALTER

Doner

Chairman & CEO

Biggest Challenges Faced

As an agency, the biggest test we face is the ability to continually recruit top-notch talent. I think the agency business has lost some of the luster, excitement, and sex appeal it had when I was growing up. The industry doesn't quite have the same stature among young people. Success is all about the people working for you - and their ideas - no matter what department they happen to represent. It has become difficult to compete for the best people in the advertising business because other industries, once considered boring and stifling, have become exciting and offer employees freedom. The elements that made advertising a good path for individuals looking to express creativity are now found in many industries.

For advertisers, the biggest challenge is no longer the talk of breaking through the clutter to create awareness and be noticed amid the recent fracturing of media. The real challenge today is being relevant. Consumers have become much smarter about their personal decisions. They are more educated today than ever before and more willing to take matters into their own hands. The Internet has changed the nature of the consumer. They've gone from being information-poor to being information rich. Consumers now control the information and make decisions regarding its use. In the end, if you aren't relevant to someone, your advertising may be consumed, but will be dismissed.

Changes Due to New Technology

I am a big believer that change is usually positive; an improvement in some way. Technology has made things easier, faster, and has provided people with more choices. The biggest impact has been the Internet empowering consumers to take things into their own hands.

When television was introduced, everyone thought radio and the movies would die; ideas that were proved wrong. People now have more media choices. The consumer loves choices and enjoys different ways of being entertained and different ways of accessing information. In addition to providing information, the Internet has changed the consumer mindset by enhancing decision-making expectations and capabilities. In the past, consumers were reactive recipients. This change will have an impact on everything we do - be it television, radio, print, or any form of one-to-one communication; because consumers now demand information choices.

Goals of an Advertising Campaign

In most cases the goal is some combination of brand health, sales of some sort, and customer loyalty. It seems to take on that progression. If you can raise brand health, you are likely to increase sales. However, you can't rely solely on brand health to reach a sales goal. If you use advertising tactics only to increase sales, then you have a brand that is in need of repair. Another goal is keeping the customer loyal. In the end, the true value of a brand is customer loyalty. If the brand fosters loyalty, it becomes stronger, more resistant to competitor attacks, and stronger among discerning consumers who will dismiss competitive claims because they believe in the brand.

Ideal Agency-Client Relationships

Two words: respect and collaboration. This goes both ways. I don't think there is a piece of magic there. I think this is the foundation for all strong relationships.

The Importance of the Creative End

After all the thinking, discussion, research, and logic that goes into a campaign, the consumer only sees the advertising. They either understand the message you are communicating or they do not. The creative is the single most important element, because the advertising is a short summary of the entire story - the part where the consumer gets to respond. Without really great creative, you are in trouble no matter how strong your core idea may happen to be.

If you can't communicate the message effectively to ensure it is not ignored or dismissed, your creative has failed. How do you go about effectively communicating the message? You rely on smart and creative people. You give them the opportunity to explore ideas that may seem on the surface crazy, wrong, or uncomfortable. In many cases, the mundane and accepted appears to be right. However, an important part of creative is being innovative; creating something that has never been seen before.

Favorite High Budget Advertising Tool

Television. It is the great communicator because it combines wonderful things. People continue to view the medium of television as the best kind of entertainment they can consume. It is incredibly powerful because you simply absorb it. It's not like reading. After television, I would say magazines. With magazines you can become extremely relevant to your audience by choosing the appropriate magazine title. You reach interested people who can be excited visually and with words. It is an interesting, challenging medium because you don't have some of the crutches available to you with television. Magazine may even be a little purer. After magazines, whatever fits the assignment or clients' needs is the next-best approach.

Staying Fresh as a Brand

I don't believe a brand should ever reinvent itself unless there is a problem. Rather, a brand should constantly refresh itself. A brand is in danger if it falls into an area of consumer familiarity where the consumer no longer listens to the message. It's a little like the house you live in. When you first move in, and decorate the house, it makes the place exciting and enjoyable. As the years go by, you don't see things anymore; not because you are bored, but because you no longer pay attention.

Changes in Advertising

I think advertising has become more difficult and will continue to get harder. We will look back at today as the good old days. Advertising has become more challenging because there is so much more pressure today for results. Often that pressure translates into lack of patience. Society today demands instant gratification. Today's technology is all about instant gratification. Society has conditioned people to expect positive reinforcement almost immediately. In this regard, instant messaging is better than email because you get an instant response. There appears to be a bit of instant gratification seeping into what marketers are expecting from advertising today. The days of building a brand have gone toward building sales.

Incorporating Discipline into Brand Communication

Refreshing a brand should not change the elements that define the brand. Likewise, communication tools should not be changed before their time. I have seen a lot of change for the sake of change as opposed to strategic change. To encourage strategic change, we identify the brand building elements versus the elements being used to build awareness in that scenario. And then we separate the two. Before anything is discarded, we analyze each element to determine whether or not it is time to refresh. The key ingredients to building the brand are not discarded or modified until it is time for them to be replaced by something else. That discipline is tough to stick with, because everyone in advertising seems to have a bit of ADD (Attention Deficit Disorder) today.

Positive Effects of Internet and Technology

We now understand who we are communicating with on a very discrete basis and have the ability to tailor communications directly to them. In direct response, we were able to tailor messages by first understanding a database and truly getting down to that level. When you combine this with the possibility of cable and the databases you can marry there, the idea of being able to create messages segmented by a database is likely to be a technology that will soon be upon us. In the past we used direct mail against slices of the consumer base. In the future, we should be able to do this with television and radio.

Future Killer Applications for Agencies

Anything that will make it easier and faster to establish and maintain a relationship with a customer will be beneficial. If you can communicate through broadband to an individual, provide them with what they are looking for, respond to them, and provide quick access to rich content, the opportunity is incredible. Right now this is primarily an advertiser-regulated communication. However, much of it will transform into a consumer-regulated communication. Broadband allows consumers to get information quickly and easily.

Wireless is going to be great. I don't think it's going to be about giving away free phones to consumers and then having the privilege to send advertising messages over that phone. The consumer doesn't want that. Rather, they want the ability to have wireless information sent to them when they need and want it. This will change the face of communication. It's a little like a dream having the television, cable, or broadcast network send me the show I want to see at 9 o'clock. We have yet to crack the code on video on demand. That will be an exciting new horizon.

Taking Advantage of New Areas as an Agency

We stay ahead of the curve in understanding, but stay on the curve in utilization. We do this because we need to know what's coming. If you use it early, it makes good news headlines and is interesting to discuss. But these types of headlines don't result in anything that's meaningful for the client. Perhaps it is better to test from time to time and see what's right for you. True utilization happens when there is a momentum in the marketplace for that new tool or killer application. That's our point of view: use it when it's going to get you the best ROI (Return On Investment). From a ROI standpoint, you don't want to be behind the curve of your competitors. It's important to be early in information and then on the curve in terms of utilization.

Major Pitfalls to Avoid

One industry pitfall is creating advertising for your peers. There is a lot of this going on. Lately, advertising has been littered with campaigns the agency holds up as great work, but the sales don't follow and the client goes out of business or hires a new agency. Everyone has fond memories of the creative advertising from the 1960's. However, that advertising always hinged on a powerful selling idea. Fast forward to the Taco Bell dog: everyone loved the dog, but no one went to the store.

Another pitfall is thinking you have found something motivating when in reality all you've found is something that the advertiser finds interesting; something the consumer doesn't find relevant. The advertiser is excited because people in the company did something or invented something they hold in high regard, but it may have no basis in consumer reality. This happens because advertisers spend a large amount of time trying to come up with some differentiating issue that has to do with technology or process. Ultimately, if it doesn't interest or excite the consumer, it's all for naught.

The Purpose of a Campaign in Terms of Investment

Everybody in the agency business likes to say that advertising is an investment, not an expense. Logic flows that if it is an investment, there has to be a return. If there is no return, it becomes an expense or a loss. The key is the timeframe in which that investment yields a return. If you return to the elements of brand health, it's going to have a return over a longer period of time. If it is measuring sales it is a rather short and defined period of time and tactical issues are used. If it is customer loyalty, it's an ongoing monitoring just how loyal your customized base is. Everything can be measured. We believe this is the correct way to apply these measurements. If you are doing something that aims to impact brand health, it is unrealistic to expect to see an ROI in thirty days. However, to say we as an agency are doing something for a client, but have no way of measuring ROI, is also unrealistic. If that's the case, why should the client invest?

Compensation for Agencies

There should be two forms of compensation. One, agencies should be paid for the work that they do - whatever that includes. Two, the agencies should also be given incentives that will reward them for success. Because what agencies do should have a positive impact on a client's business, and agencies should be held accountable for the work they do - good or bad. We should be given an incentive and be at risk. It would certainly ensure that agencies pay more attention to their clients' business if a risk/reward situation is involved, as opposed to the old days of paying 15% commission on media when it didn't matter how long the process took or how well it worked.

There aren't many agencies still working on commission. Advertisers are requiring more and more accountability within their organizations. Whether it is the General Electric process of employee evaluation or the even tougher Ford process of employee evaluation, they are demanding a lot more from each employee. I would expect them to demand the same of every vendor partner as well. The reality is that in the future every agency will be evaluated more on the contributions they make. The commission aside, I think evaluation will develop into determining how each employee affects the organization and people will be additionally compensated according to their respective contributions.

Becoming a Leader

Becoming a leader is dependent on the ability to embrace change. I think change is probably the hardest thing for people to accept because it is frightening. But a dynamic business needs to change. A leader needs to encourage trial and risk in all areas, particularly in an ad agency. The other necessary element in being a good leader is allowing people in the organization the opportunity to be in charge.

This requires finding the best people and giving them the ability to make decisions. You have to support them. We believe in providing people with maximum help and minimal interference.

Components of a Successful Advertising Team

A successful advertising team is comprised of people who respect each other and interact well together. It's a combination of sharing ideas, building on one another, supporting each other, and a willingness to embrace change. Part of change is finding the innovative solution. Too often solutions fall within a comfort zone. The real breakthrough occurs when solutions are found outside that tried-and-true comfort zone.

Retaining and Motivating Top Talent

We spend a good amount of time discussing employee retention and motivation. In the end, I believe it boils down to the organization's culture and the types of people that culture attracts. We've created an environment that makes it easy for people to buy into the agency's corporate culture. Our culture is about the freedom to do the work. We have the luxury of being a privately held company. We answer only to ourselves. This is nice. There is no holding company, no stock analyst, or stockholder. This means we have the ability to react quicker and be more responsive to the organization's needs because we don't have to stop and weigh the needs of others before we can move forward. This also means we can attract people who enjoy the responsibility that goes hand-in-hand with authority. People who enjoy a collaborative atmosphere, come to the office with a daily intensity for the business, and put pressure on one another to grow.

It isn't about the fear of the boss; it's about the expectations of all partners. This makes for a pretty motivating structure. You just have to make sure the organization is continuously delivering for the people. Too often, it becomes easy to institutionalize issues that become ingrained problems. When asked about what I do at the agency, I respond by saying that my job description is to eliminate barriers to success. The thing that usually stops good people from being successful is something standing in their way - a process, a person, a system, or a lack of technology. Those obstacles need to be removed if an agency is to be truly successful.

Keeping an Edge

Read a lot and stay current. This is sometimes a challenge and a discipline that needs to begin early in one's career. Staying current becomes more and more difficult and requires more and more effort the older we get. As we progress in life, we tend to want to stay within our comfort zones: familiar people, familiar activities, people who are like us. In order to keep an edge we need to continue to put ourselves into situations where we feel a bit uncomfortable.

The Future of Advertising

I think quite a few things will change in the next five years. One, there will be a lot more pressure for performance due to the declining state of the economy. I foresee this having an effect on agency staffing issues. Similar to what we saw in 1990, 1991, and 1992 when we experienced this pressure, the young people were cut out of the organization.

The big agencies that employ the largest staffs decided that the "expendables" were the younger people. This resulted in us waking up 10 years later to find that our mid-management ranks were vacant because that group had been eliminated by belt-tightening moves made 10 years earlier.

My fear is that the consolidation of agencies and economic pressures will result in cutbacks and inadequate training programs. The big agencies won't have as many entry-level positions and there will be fewer places for recent graduates to begin a career in advertising. We will be pushing some of the best people into other industries, and we will suffer for that five years from now.

Joining the company in 1967, Alan gained consumer and retail advertising experience overseeing a variety of agency accounts. His understanding of advertising and marketing strategies, media, direct mail, and public relations has made him an expert in the field.

Alan was named executive vice president and director of the agency's retail division in January 1990. Later that same year, he was appointed president/chief operating officer. In 1995, Alan was named chief executive officer and in 1998 became chairman of the board.

TUNING INTO THE CONSUMER

ALAN SCHULTZ

Valassis

Chairman, President & CEO

The Excitement of Advertising

The most exciting thing is creating a brand and an image for a company, product or service. Ultimately, we try and help our clients grow their business. You see a new brand grow, and you've seen that you have helped that client establish the brand image in the marketplace, which ultimately increases their sales. You watch their companies grow and they expand their facilities - that's what it is all about. We always take the approach that if it is good for our client's business, then it is good for our business, whatever that may be. Oftentimes, we will do things that aren't necessarily good for our business in the short term, but are great for the clients. We always find that, in the long run, that approach pays off.

Exciting Opportunities Going Forward

The whole concept of development of different databases that capture a tremendous amount of behavioral information about individuals and being able to use that information to better communicate, market, and build relationships with those individuals is very exciting. I think that is probably the area where you are going to see the most growth in the long run. There is a reason why companies like ENC and Oracle that are selling data storage units and software to manage data bases are growing so quickly. Everybody is in the process of building out these databases over time.

I think the world is moving through different phases. The first phase was the data phase. Now we are moving into the intelligence and information phase. We have all this data, now we have to understand what it all means in terms of information. We've moved from the data to information age. That will continue to develop. The next phase will be the knowledge phase - which is that we have all this data and information so we really have a tremendous understanding about consumers and purchase behavior. The final phase, and I definitely don't think we are anywhere near it, is the actual application phase. That is the process we are going through. That's really exciting. What really turns me on is getting into the knowledge and application phase because when we reach the application phase, that's when we really will be able to see the results.

Challenges Faced as an Advertiser

One of the biggest challenges that exist today is trying to bring all the parts together of your marketing program to synergize them. People are starting to throw out the term "convergence". What that means is that you've got all these separate sales and marketing people in different groups doing their own thing. Nobody is pulling it all together into one cohesive marketing and communication plan for the consumer. That's a big challenge and opportunity on a going forward basis.

Another huge challenge is the whole issue of media fragmentation. You've got situations now where consumers are really starting to spread their time out among a number of different media. That's making it more challenging to reach a significant number of people at one time. Quite frankly, that's one of the reasons why our mass product gets out to sixty million households a day. I think it's successful because today if you want to reach that many households in a day, your opportunities are just so limited. If you think about the fact that the Super Bowl is perceived to be the biggest media event of the year, only forty million households tune in. How do you get to a really big number of people in a short amount of time? That problem is just going to get worse as time goes on. It's a challenge today but an even larger dilemma tomorrow.

If you look at history, a hundred years ago we had newspapers. Then the radio came out on the scene, and everyone thought no one would ever buy a newspaper again when there was the radio. You could hear the information. Then came the television, and people asked why anybody would listen to the radio when you could watch television and get the picture with sound. Then the Internet came on the scene, and people said it would wipe out newspapers and television would become an interactive experience. What's happened is that the Internet has become yet another medium. Consumers now use a number of media throughout their day, rather than replacing a single medium with another.

Going forward, you have people talking about interactive television. That will become another medium. All these additional media create more fragmentation. As you get more diversity within each medium, you get even more fragmentation. Television is a great example. When you go back thirty years ago, you had three major networks that basically controlled 90% of the audience. Today, it might be 40% of the audience and there are cable stations reaching up to eighty channels. When I go up to my cabin, my satellite can reach up to six hundred channels. Marketers will have to address this issue by becoming savvier about their media mix, looking well beyond the traditional stuff of yesteryear.

Settings Goals for a Project

The start for us is always to determine what the client is trying to accomplish and what their goals and objectives are. From there, we determine how we can help clients ultimately get what they need. Success for us is helping the client. Sometimes they have short-term goals, sometimes they have long-term goals, sometimes they have goals which relate to ROI, and sometimes they have goals of awareness and image building. That's always where we start - with what the client is trying to accomplish. Then, we match up programs and services that address those needs. Rarely does one solution meet every need.

Establishing a Successful Advertising Campaign

The first thing is that the client really needs to be willing to open up and share with us all the intimacies of the business. The second thing is, from our perspective, we really have to dig in and do research to really understand their business and its challenges. Once we have done that, developing a plan or a campaign can really take many different forms. I am not sure that there is any single campaign that is ever ideal, right, or perfect. Everybody has different opinions in terms of what is the best. There is never necessarily a right or wrong answer. The one thing that is essential in all that is to have a good mix.

One of the things that concern me today is that there are companies out there selling something called "market mix modeling". Basically what they are doing is going in and doing analysis for clients. They are looking at different components of the marketing plan and trying to determine what is the "perfect" mix. Those models are very flawed and lead clients to think that one type of spending is significantly better than another type of spending. They encourage the client to take all these individual components of a marketing plan and consolidate it down to a couple of unique elements. When you water the mix down, you water the results down.

You have to have all the appropriate components. What I mean by that is that you need an advertising component that maybe includes television or radio. You need a promotional component that might include some type of call to action to really motivate the consumer (like a coupon, rebate or sweepstakes). You might need some trade dollar component if you are selling through a retail outlet to motivate the retailer. If you really have a well-designed plan, from the consumer standpoint they are getting your message from a lot of different places. That's important in a well-designed campaign. It's a three-pronged approach. One, educate consumers about your brand, and build your product's image over the long term. Two, garner retail cooperation and distribution. Three, provide incentives for the consumer to choose your brand over your competitor's.

The Importance of Creativity and Innovation

Creativity is critical. If you look at the amount of clutter that exists out there today from an advertising point of view, it becomes clear why. There has been research done on televisions, and this always fascinates me. Today, when you watch a television program, if it is an hour program, then you actually see forty-two minutes of programming and eighteen minutes worth of television commercials. You have some sets in there where sometimes you get nine to twelve commercials in a single set. The research says that by the time you get to commercial number five, there is no recall for that one or after. If you have designed a television commercial, and you are seven, eight, or nine in that set, you better have some unbelievable creativity in your commercial to get any recall from the consumer. Creativity is critical.

With that said, I do want to caution that sometimes people can get so creative that from a consumer standpoint, the consumer forgets what the product, image, and message is. One of the things I see today that is troublesome is more emphasis on creativity than brand building. Think of how many times you've been at a dinner party and someone starts talking about a great commercial they have seen on TV and then ask what product it's for. Nobody in the room can remember what the product is. That's a case where creativity has been taken to an extreme that isn't good. The other thing that is important about creativity is back to that point of convergence. You have to make sure that creativity crosses all the elements of the marketing plan. You don't see that enough.

If you look at the way clients are often structured today, they have an advertising department, advertising agency, promotion department, and promotion agency. They have one set of people filming their television commercials and another group of people designing their print ads. These people don't talk. As a result of that, each of them is trying to create their own creative one upmanship versus the other groups so that they can be sure they are more creative than the other guy. That causes the brand message to get confused and watered down. I think synergizing total marketing plans is important. There needs to be consolidation between advertising and promotion departments and agencies. You have to have a brand champion that oversees it all to protect the brand and make sure it stays consistent with the desired objectives.

The Importance of a Balanced Approach to Media

The issue starts with what the objectives are. The way you need to approach it is to be media neutral. This is one of the biggest problems with advertising agencies today. Advertising agencies are primarily incentivized on a commission basis for media that they place. The primary pairs of commission are television, radio, and magazine. As a result of that, that's where their heads are. They always start with TV because that is what is profitable for the agency. It pays the best commission and there are huge creative charges. It costs $250,000 at a minimum to shoot a commercial. So, the agency always starts out with television. If a client doesn't think television is right for their campaign, the agency goes to radio next. After radio, they go to magazines.

The reality is that there are different types of media out there that are available, like the Internet. Our company offers a lot of connective media for example. Connective media has the same image building characteristics that television, radio and magazines have. It also has a unique element associated with it, a call to action, which motivates the consumer. If you give a consumer a sample of a product and they try it, then they have connected with the brand. If you give someone a coupon or a rebate or sweepstakes offer, that is something to encourage them to get out of their chair and try the product. Many advertising agencies don't ever think of connective media as part of that media plan because the reality is that they are not media neutral. The reason for that is because of the way they are incentivized by the clients. I have always said that people will do what you pay them to do. The reality is that ad agencies get paid to produce television commercials. If they got paid to produce results for the client by building brand image and improving sales, then they would be media neutral and look at a much broader spectrum of alternatives.

The Future of Brand "Stickiness"

It's going to get a lot harder. The reason it is going to get harder is because of media fragmentation. In the time of the three major networks and 90% of the audience, a good example is Jiff Peanut butter. "Choosy mothers choose Jiff". When I was growing up as a kid, with three major networks, my father hated to watch commercials so he would change the channel whenever one came on. When you changed from ABC to NBC, you would see the same Jiff commercial. They were synchronizing them to take commercial breaks at the same time and played them at the same time. You could not avoid that commercial unless you were living in an igloo in Alaska. You could develop a campaign in which you couldn't miss as a consumer. Today, it is really easy to miss it. You have to have a broad mix to really get to everybody with the message. If you are looking at a broad based campaign, it is a huge challenge today and will be an even bigger challenge going forward.

Keeping a Brand Fresh

The most important thing is the promise. I think that for a brand to stay fresh over time, a marketer must maintain their promise of the product's quality and value. You have to fulfill the promise and stick to the commitment that you make to the consumer. You may have to revise or tweak that promise to update it to keep it contemporary, but the most important thing is that you always maintain that promise.

The other thing is that you maintain a set of loyal consumers. This is a much smaller set of consumers than what anybody wants to believe. You have to keep those loyals loyal. At the same time, you have to be bringing new people into your brand franchise. You've got your base of really solid loyal users. You have to keep those users, but continue to attract new potential users that look like them to bring them into your mix. We call it the "bucket theory". You have users in your bucket. You constantly have competitors trying to pull them out. Competitors are going to be successful pulling them out, so you have to try and keep them in, but at the same time add new people to the bucket.

Exciting Aspects of the Internet and Technology

Ultimately, what is exciting is tailoring a message to an individual consumer. The days of mass marketing programs where you can develop one message and send it to everybody are passing by. People are very unique today and have different perspectives and needs. Their needs are becoming much more narrowly focused than they ever were before. You have to communicate with different people in different ways. That's not to say you have to communicate with every single person in a unique way, but as opposed to saying you have four different marketing segments, on a going forward basis, you might have fifty different unique marketing segments, and you need to communicate with each of them on a unique basis. The complexity going forward and the marketing challenge is going to be huge compared to what it is today. The good news is that technology basically enables us to handle that complexity. Today, there is still a fair amount done in print. For example, we have some variable imaging printing capability. We have the ability to do mass customization. This means I can produce sixty thousand pieces in an hour off the end of the press. Every single one of them can be a unique piece based on someone's purchase behavior.

The Dream Advertising Tool

The dream is to communicate with someone on a one to one basis with the cost of mass distribution. People thought that was going to happen on the Internet. The idea was that the Internet was great. We could build databases on the Internet to help understand people, which led to communicating with them. The Internet is free. What people didn't understand is that the Internet may be free, but to build that database you have to go out and buy an Oracle license and get a data storage unit. Then you need programs to get the data, and to segment, analyze, and target against that data. Then you have to measure your results. The number of servers you need to communicate with people over the Internet also costs money. When the Internet first came out on the scene, I thought it was the Holy Grail. I thought it was unbelievable that you could communicate with people on a one to one basis for free. The reality is, it's not free. There is a tremendous amount of cost associated with that technology infrastructure. What will be the Holy Grail? A solution where we can communicate on a one to basis, at the cost of mass distribution.

Pitfalls to Avoid in Advertising

The thing that people, particularly creative ones, most often succumb to is to get so hung up on the creative that they forget that the objective is to sell the product. You can devise the best creative and do a phenomenal job building awareness for your product. You can have people understand what your promise is and have a clear image of what the brand is. If all that doesn't result in the sale of more product, that's probably the biggest mistake you can make.

I think another thing you need to be careful of as a marketer is to not let short-term financial objectives get in the way in doing what is right for your brand long term. You need to be skeptical of these mixed modeling techniques I discussed earlier, and have the discipline to do what's right for your brand long term. That means you need to have a balanced mix of advertising and promotion, and make every attempt to avoid slashing your marketing budget when you experience short-term market glitches.

Lastly, make sure your product can meet the claims you make in your ads – and keep those "loyals" pantries loaded.

Becoming a Leader

You have to give. To be a leader that means that you are willing to serve, whether that is serving your customers, competitors, or industry. You have to be willing to serve and do what is in the best interest of all your constituencies.

Admirable Aspects of Other Leaders

Jack Welch is an example of a great leader. I believe that most leaders develop sound strategies. Most people that rise through companies and make it to the top are bright, talented, and strategic people. They don't fail because they have a poor strategy but because of execution problems. The challenge is to bring your company along and get them to understand, embrace, and execute your strategy. That's what separates the great leaders from the good leaders.

Building a Successful Advertising Team

I think you need a cross section of people. That's important. The obvious one is that you need the creative people, communications, public relations, and marketing people. Those are all the obvious ones. People often forget that legal counsel is good to have. Having someone from the finance side is important to make sure you are doing things that fit within the budget. If you are looking for positive ROI, you can actually measure it after the fact. Operational people are important. Everybody tends to be specialized these days and tends to focus on different areas. The greater cross section of people you have participating in the process, the greater number of perspectives you have. The more perspectives you have, the better the results. Diversity is an important issue, particularly with the changing face of America. You see explosive growth in the Hispanic population, a large African American population, and a growing Asian population. You need a multicultural participation also.

People that lead by example and don't ask someone to do something they are not willing to do themselves stand out. You need personable people who can empathize with other people, understand their situation, relate to it, and want to help. One of the concepts that we talked about is building social capital whether that is with your clients or employees. My definition of social capital is that you know when you have it when people want to help you and be successful. If you can build that social capital and have people working for you who want to see you win, that's pretty powerful.

Keeping Your Edge as an Advertiser

You have to do a combination of things. You have to be well read whether it is magazines, books, industry articles, or research. Those are all important elements. You have to participate in industry associations to find out what the latest and greatest is. You have to be out with your clients. Client participation is key - what are the challenges, problems, needs, and wants. You have to be out there with those customers to be current.

The Future of Advertising

I think you are going to see agencies become media neutral. Clients are going to require that. You are going to see dramatic change in the way agencies operate. You will also see television start to have some long-term problems. The fragmentation and costs have reached the point where television is as popular as it is going to be. It's not going to be cost justified. With the remote control taken to the next step with V chips, within the next five years people will be able to tune out intrusive advertising. You will need to advertise to people in a way that they want to receive it. It needs to be welcomed into the home. Consumers are becoming more demanding and more sophisticated, and both advertising messages and media choices will need to rise to a new level to connect with them.

Alan F. Schultz is president and chief executive officer at Valassis (NYSE: VCI) and is also chairman of VCI's board of directors. In his position as president and CEO, Schultz heads up the VCI leadership team, which is responsible for the development of growth strategies and new business opportunities, as well as overseeing the day-to-day operations of the company.

In his former position as executive vice president and chief operating officer, Schultz was responsible for leading many of the company's recent successful ventures. He played a key role in the launch of VCI's sampling division, was instrumental in the development of the company's targeting services, and has also spearheaded recent industry initiatives which have aided in growing the FSI industry.

Schultz joined Valassis in 1984 after working as a CPA for Deloitte & Touche. Since then, he has lead many different areas of the company, such as finance and operations, marketing, and sales.

UNDERSTANDING THE CLIENT PERSPECTIVE

BRENDAN RYAN
Foote, Cone & Belding Worldwide
(FCB Worldwide)
CEO

Advertising Expertise

This business requires a combination of skills that don't normally show up in one person. Engineers are good at engineering, accountants are good at accounting. In this business, particularly if you are on the management side, you need a couple of things. I start with the fact that I love advertising. I think I am very good at looking at storyboards, film, or thinking about a product and coming up with an avenue to advertise it in. You've got to really like ads. I never understand why people come into this business if they don't love ads. I love to sit and look at ads and talk about how we can make them better with other people. So you have to be good at advertising.

Then you combine that with being good with people and clients. A great advantage I have is that I used to be a client. That's a huge advantage, because I understand the pressures clients are under. You have to be able to connect with senior clients about their business from their perspective and then help them understand how advertising can help them achieve their goals. Fundamentally, you must be good at ads and at understanding your clients' business, understanding them as people, and causing them to follow your lead and recommendations in a situation where you are not the boss.

Those are two fundamental skills. You need others, depending on what your job is. Leadership is essential. You have to be someone whom people will follow. When people ask me what is different about leading an agency versus being a client, one of the key differences is the diversity of people that you lead in the agency. On some days it seems as if no two people in the agency have a similar view of life. It's really a challenge to constantly keep that crowd flying in some semblance of formation and to feel good about what we are doing as an agency. We want to cause people to work here. One of the central issues of our industry today is attracting and keeping the best people. Money and good stock do help, but at the end of the day, people in this business want a place where they like going to work every day. The best people have the option of changing to another place easily if they don't like where they are.

Surprising Aspects on the Agency Side

There are a couple of things as a client that you don't appreciate. One is how capable some people in the agency are regardless of what position they are in. Some of the smartest and most astute business people are some of the flakiest writers you might run into. Appearances can be very deceiving. The amount of effort in what goes into developing a simple thing like a thirty-second commercial is immense, in terms of research, insight, thinking, strategy, confronting a blank page, and coming up with ideas. Then, the amount of detail that goes into producing a thirty-second commercial is also staggering. As a client, you sit there and see a finished product of a thirty-second film, but there is so much that underlies what you don't see.

It's also a very different management model. Client companies tend to be more like a military model. You are the colonel, he's the captain so he does what you tell him. In an agency we have a much flatter structure and a lot of people in this business think that they are in charge of everything. They are not, but that's another story. Leadership and management is much more using persuasion than giving commands.

Changes in the Advertising World

I held an FCB Senior Management meeting just two years ago, and it is extraordinary how many things have changed since then. The biggest changes that I see affecting our business are those affecting clients. The increasing pressure on clients to deliver immediate business results has, in turn, put great pressure on agencies. The focus on what we do now has to be on generating immediate sales and profit for our clients. This has therefore caused agencies to look to ways to heighten the odds of success with things like direct and interactive marketing to deliver immediate results. You see agencies going beyond thirty-second commercials to include other channels. The ability to help lay out a plan for those clients as to how to allocate spending across all channels is becoming more central to what we do.

Big Issues Moving Forward

The fundamental principle that underlies advertising is to "run effective advertising; sell more products; make more profit". Over time you will hopefully build your brand, which lets you charge more for the product. I think credibility in this premise is eroding. I believe too few clients today look at advertising as a short-term cure for sales weakness. But, if you accept that, it says to me that we've got to focus on developing ads that have as their objective selling something and building the brand, in that order.

In addition, we have to start taking better advantage of additional weapons to get consumers to use our products. We need to blend together traditional direct marketing along with interactive marketing using database techniques to really help us oversee that entire combination of spending. We have got to continue to deliver excellence in creativity in traditional advertising. But now we have to offer it through those other channels, as well. If we don't, we will die.

Establishing Successful Advertising Campaigns

We have to get even better at identifying target audiences, and understanding their attitudes, behaviors, and perspectives towards the product. In turn, this should lead to better understanding of who our copy writers are trying to communicate with. This, then, should lead to more targeted and meaningful advertising, which then should lead to media vehicles that are chosen on more relevant criteria. The days of carpet-bombing America with thirty-second commercials are going to end. The opportunity to focus messages from a content and media vehicle standpoint is going to really increase. That will heighten the odds of advertising being effective in the sense of generating profit for the clients.

Measures of Success for an Advertising Campaign

The traditional measures have been fundamentally soft. Advertising has traditionally been measured on things like awareness, brand preference and attitudes, but that is no longer enough. There are techniques coming along every day that are increasingly sophisticated and accurate at measuring the real impact of advertising. Using database marketing, we have invented a product called "Prophesy", which quantitatively and on an ROI basis measures the effectiveness of marketing spending across several different channels, including advertising. It gives very specific recommendations to clients as to how to allocate their money by measuring ROI. It actually really works.

More and more, accurate measurement is where we have to head. One, it clearly supports the view that advertising works. Two, it enables an agency to generate better compensation for itself because you can demonstrably point to results. No client is going to be angry about giving you more money as an incentive payment if you can show that you have dramatically increased his or her profits.

Making a Campaign Stand out Creatively

I don't separate creativity from effectiveness. I think this nonsense that you read about today about what is creative, often has nothing to do with whether it has sold anything or not. I am the first guy to want creativity because that is what is at the heart of what we do. That's what we bring to the party. But at the end of it all, don't tell me something is an admired commercial because of its creativity when you can't even tell me what the product is. There is a lot of that today.

Advertising is not about entertaining, it's about entertaining with a purpose. I think it is ever more challenging to us in our business to be "creative". It is essential that the advertisement makes you pause and cause you to think about something. But if there is no "rock in the snowball" or something important to the viewer that leads one to the product, you are kidding yourself and wasting your time. The client shouldn't keep spending money.

Learning From Campaigns

It is essential to learn from everything you do. It is ridiculous to make the same mistake more than once. For example, immediately after we shoot a commercial, we sit down with the writer, art director, film producer, planner and client and look them over to understand, if we were doing them again, what we would do differently. You have to make sure you constantly look over stuff to make it better. Once you do something, you learn from it and keep trying to improve it.

Changes in the Level of Advertising

Advertising has gotten harder. Within product categories, there often isn't really a meaningful difference between products. To advertise a product where there is some immensely compelling benefit is pretty easy. We'd love to say: "Drink this soda, lose twenty pounds". That would be an easy sell but that's not the way it is most of the time. Coming up with an insight about a product and then turning it into something magical is very difficult.

Creating Environments for Magical Moments

Fundamentally finding the magic moment is about the atmosphere you set, and what the leadership of the agency deems important and lets the rest of the world know is important. It's about giving people the freedom to swing for big ideas. It's about causing clients to trust you and let you take that big swing on the campaign idea. It's really having an ability to develop insights about the brand and the consumer. If you have the right insight, you really have a great chance of getting a great campaign. If you don't have the insight, the odds are very much longer.

Creating a Bond With the Client

You have to learn their business, and know their business as well as they do. You have to help them to understand how much you care about their business, and then work your way down from that level of trust to being able to deliver the goods. You have to be the guy at the agency who causes the best people at the agency to want to work on your client's business. When you are known as that kind of person, clients trust you a lot and you get a lot of leeway.

Importance of the Internet

The Internet is getting there, but perhaps slower than most would have anticipated. It is a very big part of FCB's offering right now, and is very much how we will measure the effectiveness of our efforts. As an advertising vehicle, however, it has not been terribly effective. Banners and other online programs have not been a great idea. Where the Internet could become hugely critical would be in enabling us to identify specific customers, to understand their characteristics, and to reach them very directly. And broadband is critical to that future. Both broadband and wireless, I think, will be big, but broadband will be much bigger than wireless. There are those who say that some day when you walk down the street and pass a shoe store, you will see advertisement for it on your cell phone. I don't know, I am not counting on that.

Major Pitfalls to Avoid

Don't over-promise. Don't treat people like morons. Don't be too cute and precious. If you have something to say, say it clearly, don't let the execution overpower what you are trying to say. Don't build bridges halfway across the lake. Let's say you've got four or five different brands in your division and you only have money for two of them. Don't spend your money for all five, focus it on the two best opportunities.

Becoming a Leader in the Advertising World

You must demonstrate a keen willingness to do it. It is a long, hard job. You get a lot of people that want a piece of you - a lot of clients, and a lot of employees. You have to make a strong commitment. You have to love what you do. You don't want to fool people. If you fundamentally don't like advertising or the people that work in it, why continue? You should celebrate victories a lot. You have to communicate a lot. If you are the kind of person that likes to barricade yourself in the office, this isn't the right kind of job for you. It is a business of walking halls, visiting offices, countries and clients. You have to be on the move a lot. You write a lot, send out a lot of letters.

Becoming a successful manager depends on your job. I am the CEO so I have a major financial responsibility here to deliver agreed-upon profit targets. I dislike the "vision" word, but I have to be able to lay out a view of what we are going to accomplish and why we are the right firm to do it for a client. That's a key piece. We have to lead by example. People who don't work hard in this business are not going to be successful.

Another important characteristic is resiliency. Advertising as a career versus being a client is that the highs are higher, the lows are lower, and there are lots more of both. I have a good day, a bad day, and I have to be able to deal with that. You have to be able to handle being tossed down unfairly by a client one day, and be able to pitch another one the next day.

Establishing a Vision

I am not a vision guy with mission statements all over the wall. I generally find there is an inverse correlation between the length of the mission statement on the wall and the people understanding what the heck it says. You start by figuring out what the essence of the business is. In my case it is about clients. Why are clients hiring agencies? You have to talk to enough of them to get a clear view of what they are looking for from their agency. To be successful you need to provide that better than any of the other agencies. The degree to which you can articulate what is needed and are able to prescribe it and deliver it, will decide if you are going to be successful.

Admirable Aspects of Other Advertisers

I like guys who are down to earth and who have integrity. I like people who get it, who don't give you ten pages of bullshit as opposed to a page of bullet points that make sense. I like people who are enthusiastic about the business and about ads, who love talking about them, and have some fun in the office - as opposed to people who are endlessly telling you bad news with no solution in sight.

Keeping an Edge

Much of it is common sense, it's not book learning. You always try to react to advertising as a consumer. I look at advertising every month - all the tapes are sent to me from our offices around the world. I look at them and send back my feedback. It keeps me on top of what we do.

I love TV, but I don't watch PBS, I watch the sitcoms. If you are going to be an advertiser, you have to be in tune with your culture and know what is going on. To be successful you have to even be a bit ahead of your culture. If you are lagging behind, you are out of it, but if you go too far out front, nobody knows what you are doing. It is important to go to movies, read lots of books, and read magazines like *People* and *Rolling Stone*. That is very important. Not enough people do, and when they sit down to assess a script or commercial they are unqualified because they don't know in what context it is going to run.

Characteristics of a Successful Advertising Team

It is a tough business. You need people who are intellectually curious, realistic, get what the point of it is, who can look at the world through a different lens and bring a different perspective, and who can articulate and execute in a way to accomplish a business purpose. That comes back to leadership skills that include being articulate, talking straightforwardly, and being able to write. Within the agency, you can really afford to only have good people.

The Future of Advertising

I think it is going to become more focused, more targeted, and will use more diverse channels of communication. Advertising is going to be a term that will apply equally to things we do on the Web as well as things we do in television. Ironically, we are going to broaden the way we communicate and narrow the targets that we talk to because we will be able to understand our consumers better and reach them more precisely.

Confounding the predictions of his eighth grade teacher and the Kuder Preference test, which indicated that he was best suited to be a short-order cook, Brendan has been Chief Executive Officer of FCB Worldwide since March '96. He is also a member of the Board of Directors of True North Communications. For the prior five years, Brendan was President, CEO of FCB New York which grew roughly from $500 million in annual billings to over $1 billion.

Before joining FCB, Brendan spent 14 years at Ogilvy & Mather, where his principal responsibilities involved heading up the American Express and Kraft Foods accounts on a global basis. In addition, he was a member of the Board of Directors of OMW and head of the Account Management Department in New York.

Before Ogilvy & Mather, Brendan spent almost ten years in Product Development at General Foods, where he claims to have invented Stove Top Stuffing. He also spent two years at Citibank as Vice President of Marketing, where he claims to have learned how to balance his checkbook.

RELEVANCE AND RESULTS IN THE AGE OF THE INTERNET

DAVID KENNY

Digitas

Chairman & CEO

What is the Internet?

There are many misconceptions about just what the Internet is. Let me begin this chapter by being very clear about what it is not. As most companies have learned the hard way, the Internet is not a vehicle for generating income. In any given month, half of the largest U.S. consumer business sites generate no commercial revenue.

It is not a low-cost way to acquire new customers. In fact, companies that use standard "drive-to-site" Web marketing, such as those ubiquitous banner ads, soon discover that their customer acquisition costs are one to two times greater than non-Web-based acquisition methods. It is not an easy method for capturing customer data. From our estimates, those sites that do take a stab at gathering self-reported data wind up with meaningful profiles on fewer than 1% of their customers.

So what, then, is all the hoopla about? Given that the Internet has been a staggering disappointment for corporate America who, by the way, invested $10 billion in Web site development in 1999, wouldn't we all be better off cutting our losses, licking our wounds and going back to the old way of doing things?

In a word: No. Because the Internet has changed everything. And it has changed everything in a really big way. To understand just how much, think on the scale of how electricity and railroads and air travel have transformed the way we think, the way we behave, the way we live our day-to-day lives. The Internet is revolutionary on a similar scale, and we've just barely begun to tap its potential.

And when I say "potential", I mean the promise of connecting with customers as never before, and doing it in such a way that the connection is not only welcomed by the consumer, but sought after. It is the promise of companies and customers entering into long-term partnerships that are mutually beneficial. And yes, that means profitable. Because advertising in the Internet age will be very much about accountability. Whereas today firms are known primarily for their creative work, it is becoming increasingly important for that creative work to yield strong results. Very soon, a campaign's return on investment will stand on the same platform as creativity, use of technology and all the other benchmarks currently used to judge the leaders in this industry. The great campaigns, and the great firms, will be those that combine creativity and technology in a way that is of true benefit to the customer. Therein lies the challenge and the opportunity of the Internet age.

What the Internet Is Now

The majority, the great majority, of destination Web sites fail because they do not fit either the needs of the companies or their customers. It's a bit of a chicken and egg problem, in that the sites don't provide enough value to bring consumers back time and again, disclosing more and more information about themselves each time; and because the customers don't come back often, the company can't develop a profile on them that is meaningful enough to enable them to develop the deep, ongoing relationships necessary to justify the high cost of building the site in the first place.

But, despair not. There is a solution, and it lies in companies making the leap from merely creating a Web site to doing the hard work necessary to develop an Internet strategy. Most companies have made the mistake that the two are synonymous, when in truth they are anything but. Confusing Web sites with the Internet is kind of like confusing light bulbs with electricity. The light bulb was just the first application. Electricity was rolled out and innovated over time. It didn't happen immediately, and the same thing is true of the Internet. Information is now being disseminated to every point of transaction and information is coming back from every transaction into central databases. Customer experiences are being untethered from the product and distribution channels that have framed them in the past. We are evolving toward a universe of ubiquity, where parallel interactions will be facilitated by a single identifying characteristic. It can be a PIN, a fingerprint, a retinal print, a laser ID. The delivery mechanism is almost inconsequential to the strategic intent of the market opportunity because we are able to reach customers at every touch point: in the home, on the road or at the point-of-sale. In just a few years (for certain fewer than five), the Internet will begin to be accessible from just about anywhere. And I do mean anywhere. Your kitchen, your car, your local coffee shop.

Technology is moving away from being Web site centric to actually wiring people across every point of contact. There's much more integration between Internet technologies and call centers. There's much more integration of Internet technologies to point-of-sale. I'm sure you're starting to see it when you're checking into hotels. You'll increasingly see it as you check in at an airline counter. You're going to increasingly see it at retail. In fact, the databases behind the Internet are fundamentally what are going to drive people to more and more specific direct marketing programs.

Soon a large portion of the population will be connected and wired to some Internet virtually every waking hour of the day. Some things like program trading will actually be set up so people are wired to the Web 24 hours a day. Once people are connected and carrying the Web with them in a ubiquitous way, we're going to go back to pure direct marketing skills, honing our knowledge of how to deliver the right message to each customer through the right channel at the right time to facilitate a sale and build a relationship.

What we're evolving toward, in essence, is a marriage of the promise of target marketing with the promise of mobile access. With mobile access comes a fundamental shift in the customer's relationship with a marketer, a fundamental shift in customer expectations and use models, and a marked increase in the opportunities for relationship building and contextual marketing.

With new technologies, the end game shifts from driving the customer to a Web site. The focus, instead, is reaching the customer precisely at the point of need. The immediacy, and the customer intimacy, is key. And this is where the direct marketing professional has a distinct and compelling competitive advantage. We're not bombarding the customer with product messages. Rather, we're facilitating customer need and desire. Think about this for a moment. It represents a radical shift in the way many advertisers view themselves. It is not about bombarding people with messages and hoping they respond. We've seen that this approach is not effective anyway. The average click-through rate of traditional banner ads is in the low single digits, and dropping, as people learn to tune out the banners much as they tune out ads on television and radio. It is about providing a service that is needed and welcomed. Imagine the customer relationship building potential of this new mindset.

It's About the Customer

Advertisers and the companies for whom they work like to think that through advertising, they are engaging in a conversation with their customers. But for the most part, the conversation is one-sided. That's because traditional advertising, however clever, is product-centric. But the ubiquitous Internet is changing all that.

I believe we are today at the very early stage of a long-term transformation in the way business is done. We are evolving toward a world in which the most effective advertising is customer-centric, not product-centric, where customers actually invite select advertisers to engage in a transaction-driven dialogue, where the objective is not so much call-to-action as it is to fulfill an immediate customer need or desire.

Rather than struggling to attract people to a destination, the extraordinary reach of the Internet can be used to deliver messages and information tailored to the customers' needs and interests, and that information can be delivered to those customers right at the point of need. This is what we call contextual marketing, and it has all the brilliance of a light bulb with even more of the staying power.

As the Internet does become ubiquitous, think of the tremendous marketing opportunities for companies to connect with their customers on an ongoing basis. Mobile devices and Internet access in a broad range of public venues allows contextual marketers to link real-life situations to virtual information and offerings. Time-sensitive contextual promotions can influence customer-purchasing decisions. They also allow companies to vary their pricing in real time in response to market and supply conditions.

Imagine being able to respond not only to who your customer is, but also to where she is and what she is doing - at that moment. Getting it right entails mastering a new way of thinking, shifting to a service orientation that can recognize and anticipate the customers needs and fulfill them at the most opportune time.

For retailers, mobile devices can identify loyal customers digitally as soon as they enter the store, and the retailer can offer on-the-spot specials based on the customer's known preferences. Airlines are another example: Of course customers use the airline Web sites to make travel reservations and check schedules, but the ubiquitous Internet allows for so much more. If the plane is delayed or rerouted, hotels, restaurants and car rental companies can respond to the customer's changing needs.

This is a whole lot more complex than simply building a Web site. Those companies that master it will be able to charge a premium, because they will not be seen as offering a product, they will be seen as offering a service, fulfilling the customer's need right at the point of need. It is the classic marketing goal of delivering the right product to the right customer at the right time, but the ubiquitous Internet provides a far superior delivery system. The "four Ps" of traditional marketing that we all learned in Marketing 101 - price, product, placement and promotion - still apply, but in an ever-changing way, based on the customer and the customer's context.

What is Old is New Again

As our understanding of the Internet matures, as we move beyond thinking about it as a utility to understanding in terms of information, we are opening whole new areas for digital interaction, triggering a shift in the traditional marketing paradigm from content to context. We're talking about understanding the customer in a context that allows us, as marketers, to connect with considerably more pull than push. Because that understanding of context allows us to create value for the customer, in a particular place, at a particular time.

Online, we have the ability to create communities as they once were, in the time before advertising. Back then, people identified themselves in terms of the community to which they belonged, whether it be their religion, university or town or country of origin.

Later, traveling salespeople entered a community with a catalog of products and became part of the town's fabric. As consumers entered into a buying contract with that salesperson, an interactive community of sellers and buyers developed. This sense of community deteriorated when more modern, passive forms of advertising kicked in during the 20th century. With television and radio, the audience is passive, sitting there receiving a message or, in all likelihood, tuning it out and not receiving it at all.

But the beauty and the challenge of the Internet is that it is an active medium in which advertisers must entice consumers to participate in a marketing strategy. And the correct way to do this is to find a way or, ideally, several ways, to put themselves between the consumers and their needs, much like a skilled traveling salesman of old would take the time up front to divine a customer's personal interests and needs, and use all the skills and resources at his disposal to close the sale.

In that sense, what is old is new again. The customer is once again in charge, and it is up to the salesman (read: marketer) to do the due diligence necessary to increase his chances of closing the sale.

Let's go back to what we learned in that Marketing 101 class and see a few examples of how the concepts of price, product, placement and promotion can be executed in new ways:

Price: For a long distance carrier, the challenge was to help them win back the price-sensitive customers they had lost to aggressive competitors. Early on, we developed a complex segmentation strategy that allowed us to focus on high leverage areas and profitable customers. Over time, we continued to refine that segmentation to include more sophisticated variables, such as behavioral and cultural elements. As the segments have become more complex, the strategy evolved, ultimately enabling the long distance carrier to offer different pricing packages to different consumers based on individual needs and profitability models. Our measurement of the program's results has also evolved. In the early stages, we viewed sales as the primary barometer of success. Performance metrics today include not just program and segment profitability calculations but also customer-level data.

Product: An international financial services firm charged us with corralling the abundance of financial information and sifting through and translating that information in a way that would match clients' interests and help them profit from market opportunities. Because information on Wall

Street is akin to currency, the information had to be delivered at market-beating speed. We designed a system that delivered aggregated, distilled market information to relationship managers. We then used integrated Web connectivity to build a high-speed CRM system to bring highly personalized, valuable information from disparate sources to a single screen. The system made it possible for relationship managers to respond to the individual needs of their clients at remarkable speed, providing superior customer service at enhanced levels of profitability.

Placement: When a major airline charged us with increasing its customer base, we spent considerable time up front getting to know the existing customers. We discovered that over one million of the airlines' frequent flyers were avid golfers, and that avid golfers, as it turned out, flew 62% more segments and generated 66% more revenue than non-golfers. On top of that, we discovered 5 million golfers lived in one of the airline's hub cities but were not regular customers. All successful marketing begins with knowing who your customers are and targeting those customers. We did just that. Using this information, we used golf as the backbone for a loyalty incentive program aimed at rewarding existing customers and enticing new ones. The email and direct mail promotions achieved a very high success rate, simply because they were tied directly to the consumers' interests.

Promotion: One luxury carmaker had a hit on its hands: 74% of test drives resulted in vehicle purchase within one year. But despite these extraordinary results, the brand had a low level of awareness in its class. Our objective was to raise that awareness and generate profitable leads for dealers. Our initial effort was online. We identified prospects in places others might not expect to find them - sites such as epicurious.com and concierge.com - and combined the luxury test drive experience with a high-end travel and leisure hook that generated so many leads it exceeded expectations by 400%. More importantly, we used the findings from that campaign to develop a fully integrated, multi-channel campaign that was even more targeted. The hook again was based on lifestyle, this time involving the Montreux Jazz Festival in Switzerland. The result: we exceeded expectations by 464% and more than doubled the number of qualified prospects we were able to drive to dealers. The return on investment for this work was significantly above expectations.

The key in each of these examples was getting the right message to the right target at the right time. Critical to that was finding the correct community and embedding ourselves in it.

What the Internet Will Be

No one would argue that contextual marketing is coming. But the truth is, we are not entirely sure what it will look like, how well it will work and how it will be used. I've taken some stabs at predicting here, but it is the marketplace that will decide. And the marketplace is anything but predictable. Experts told us television would change the way children are educated. They were right, but not in they way they'd hoped, as kids today spend more time watching "trash TV" than they spend on homework.

But I, for one, am fascinated and excited by the vast unknown of the Internet. Yes, we do know that this new technology will allow us to use our TV remote control to order an article of clothing worn by a television personality, but this is trivial compared to what the possibilities are. And the possibilities are nothing short of magic.

But how to convey this to skeptical clients, many of who were burned with massive Web site investments that often fizzled, then failed? You can't blame them for perhaps wanting to step away from the table for a while, to see how this new idea of the ubiquitous Internet will play out.

We tell our clients that the age of ubiquity is something that cannot be ignored. It is coming to America, and it's already arrived in Japan. Wireless carrier NTT DoCoMo signed up 10 million consumers for its i-mode service, which offers subscribers wireless access to thousands of services. There are now close to 10,000 i-mode sites, with more being developed every day.

And then we remind our clients that if they can add true value to their customers' lives, their relationships with those customers will benefit. Companies that anticipate and meet the real needs of their customers, and who do it based on where they are and what they are doing, will achieve the coveted status of valued partner, as opposed to pesky marketer. It is a distinction that comes with a huge return on investment.

Success in this New Age

Success in this new environment is not about marketing and it is not about technology. It is about both, in equal measure. Digitas wouldn't be able to do the degree of customer–based management and spot-on marketing that we do without having the technology. And our technology is differentiated because it's rooted in a marketing strategy. We understand how customers are going to use it. It's not just technology for its own sake.

The Yin and Yang of marketing and technology have to work together; it's essential that we show a healthy respect in both directions. There is great skepticism that both cultures can coexist in most companies. But look at the great companies out there right now and you'll see that they position themselves as both marketing and technology companies. And when I speak about Digitas, fifty percent of the time I say "We're a technology and marketing company", and the other half of the time I say, "We're a marketing and technology company". I make a point to switch the order around. It is a way for me to remind myself that one is no more important than the other. They are both critical, and I think it is the model for the winning companies of the next economy.

Mass marketers need to transition - and quickly - into direct marketers. The winners will develop database-marketing tools that will allow them to target messages in real time. They will create the middleware that will enable them to tailor messages to customers' ever-changing needs. And they will adopt the discipline of measurement. They will understand more than attitudes. They will understand behavior. And the winners will be willing to think big thoughts. We are amazed in our work by the number of Fortune 500 company executives that think of the Internet as a vehicle for judicious experimentation. Particularly in industries characterized by channel warfare, managements have a tendency to see the Internet in the context of what it can do to protect the core franchise. And while the Web can be effective at deepening relationships with existing customers and leveraging existing assets, it can only be so when it is part of a contextual marketing strategy that takes into account the customer's needs, and all the different venues the customer now has for fulfilling those needs. In short, winners in this new environment will be those who aren't afraid to think big and act big. With the customer now in control, they will admit into their lives only those messages that are relevant to their lives. The equation is simple: Does the information add value or does it not? It is the challenge of the new age to determine just what that value is (and it will change for each and every customer), and to then deliver that value through the right channel at the right time. It is a huge task, and getting it right will require a skill set different from what now exists in most firms.

Future Advertisers of America

Advertising has always attracted the smart, the strategic, the creative, the curious, the warm and the witty - people who live every day secure in the knowledge that brevity is the soul of wit, and who can say in seconds what others need hours to communicate.

I like to think that those characteristics will continue to define people in the advertising industry, with a few additions. Advertising is already attracting professionals who only recently might not have given it much thought: engineers and technologists, for example, who are able to take the technical and translate it into a sublime customer experience. This technical expertise - in the areas of hardware, software, database, research and design - is critical to making it all work. But the even greater need, as I see it, is for very smart people with merchant mentality. We need problem solvers of the highest order; people who have the mental agility to understand and utilize the ubiquitous opportunities, and who are also verbal enough and persuasive enough to translate the complexity with passion to clients. Like the very best athletes, they tend to be good at all sports. And like the very best musicians, they tend to play many instruments.

And Remember That It All Comes Down to Results

Accountability matters more than it ever has before. So much of the focus in the advertising industry has been on the creative awards, on the work versus the result. But in the digital age, the sales results will be increasingly important to the way we brand. We're going to be known by our results.

In fact, if I were to choose one watchword for the new age, I would choose "results". Because success in the future will be driven not by the masses but by the minutiae. By the ability to use technology and information to create value at the point of need. By the ability to use information to shape more than attitudes - to shape behavior. And to do it in such a way that we achieve exponentially improved levels of customer satisfaction and business results. The proof, of course, will come with time. Because no matter what the delivery method, be it the door-to-door salesman, a paper catalog or a wireless application, costs must be covered before profits can be made.

As Chairman and Chief Executive Officer of Digitas, David Kenny is one of the chief architects of global e-business transformation in the Age of the Internet. With perspective and insight, he has earned a coveted role as strategic partner to some of the world's most respected corporations, including American Express, AT&T, General Motors, Charles Schwab, Delta Air Lines, FedEx, Kingfisher, L.L. Bean, Morgan Stanley, and the National Basketball Association.

A former senior partner at Bain & Company, the global strategic consulting firm, Mr. Kenny holds a BS from the General Motors Institute and an MBA from the Harvard Business School. He is Chairman of the Board of Teach for America and a director of The

Corporate Executive Board. He is also an active member of the BOLD Diversity Initiative.

Inside the Minds: Leading Advertisers

Industry Leaders Share Their Knowledge on the Future of Building Brands Through Advertising – *Inside the Minds: Leading Advertisers* features CEOs/Presidents from agencies such as Young & Rubicam, Leo Burnett, Ogilvy, Saatchi & Saatchi, Interpublic Group, Valassis, Grey Global Group and FCB Worldwide. These leading advertisers share their knowledge on the future of the advertising industry, the everlasting effects of the Internet and technology, client relationships, compensation, building and sustaining brands, and other important topics.

Inside the Minds: Leading Consultants

Industry Leaders Share Their Knowledge on the Future of the Consulting Profession and Industry - *Inside the Minds: Leading Consultants* features leading CEOs/Managing Partners from some of the world's largest consulting companies. These industry leaders share their knowledge on the future of the consulting industry, being an effective team player, the everlasting effects of the Internet and technology, compensation, managing client relationships, motivating others, teamwork, the future of the consulting profession and other important topics.

Inside the Minds: Leading CEOs

Industry Leaders Share Their Knowledge on Management, Motivating Others, and Making a Difference At Any Level Within an Organization - *Inside the Minds: Leading CEOs* features some of the biggest name, proven CEOs in the world. These highly acclaimed CEOs share their knowledge on management, the Internet and technology, client relationships, compensation, motivating others, building and sustaining a profitable business and making a difference at any level within an organization.

Inside the Minds: Internet Marketing

Industry Experts Reveal the Secrets to Marketing, Advertising, and Building a Successful Brand on the Internet - *Inside the Minds: Internet Marketing* features leading marketing VPs from some of the top Internet companies in the world including Buy.com, 24/7 Media, DoubleClick, Guerrilla Marketing, Viant, MicroStrategy, MyPoints.com, WineShopper.com, Advertising.com and eWanted.com. Their experiences, advice, and stories provide an unprecedented look at the various online and offline strategies involved with building a successful brand on the Internet for companies in every industry. Also examined is calculating return on investment, taking an offline brand online, taking an online brand offline, where the future of Internet marketing is heading, and numerous other issues.

Inside the Minds: Internet Bigwigs

Industry Experts Forecast the Future of the Internet Economy - *Inside the Minds: Internet Bigwigs* features a handful of the leading minds of the Internet and technology revolution. These individuals include executives from Excite (Founder), Beenz.com (CEO), Organic (CEO), Agency.com (Founder), Egghead (CEO), Credite Suisse First Boston (Internet Analyst), CIBC (Internet Analyst) and Sandbox.com. Items discussed include killer-apps for the 21st century, the stock market, emerging industries, international opportunities, and a plethora of other issues affecting anyone with a "vested interest" in the Internet and technology revolution.

Bigwig Briefs: Management & Leadership
Industry Experts Reveal the Secrets How to Get There, Stay There, and Empower Others That Work For You

Bigwig Briefs: Management & Leadership includes knowledge excerpts from some of the leading executives in the business world. These highly acclaimed executives explain how to break into higher ranks of management, how to become invaluable to your company, and how to empower your team to perform to their utmost potential. (102 Pages) $14.95

Bigwig Briefs: Human Resources & Building a Winning Team
Industry Experts Reveal the Secrets to Hiring, Retaining Employees, Fostering Teamwork, and Building Winning Teams of All Sizes

Bigwig Briefs: Human Resources & Building a Winning Team includes knowledge excerpts from some of the leading executives in the business world. These highly acclaimed executives explain the secrets behind hiring the best employees, incentivizing and retaining key employees, building teamwork, maintaining stability, encouraging innovation, and succeeding as a group. (102 Pages) $14.95

Bigwig Briefs: The Golden Rules of the Internet Economy
Industry Experts Reveal the Best Advice Ever on Succeeding in the Internet Economy

Bigwig Briefs: The Golden Rules of the Internet Economy includes knowledge excerpts from some of the leading business executives in the Internet and Technology industries. These highly acclaimed executives explain where the future of the Internet economy is heading, mistakes to avoid for companies of all sizes, and the keys to long term success. (102 Pages) $14.95

Bigwig Briefs: Startups Keys to Success
Industry Experts Reveal the Secrets to Launching a Successful New Venture

Bigwig Briefs: Startups Keys to Success includes knowledge excerpts from some of the leading VCs, CEOs CFOs, CTOs and business executives in every industry. These highly acclaimed executives explain the secrets behind the financial, marketing, business development, legal, and technical aspects of starting a new venture. (102 Pages) $14.95

Bigwig Briefs: Small Business Internet Advisor
Industry Experts Reveal the Secrets to Internet Marketing, BizDev, HR, Financing, eCommerce and Other Important Topics Facing Every Small Business Doing Business on the Internet

Bigwig Briefs: Small Business Internet Advisor includes knowledge excerpts from some of the leading executives in the world in every field of specialty. These highly acclaimed executives explain the secrets behind making the most of your small business online in a very easy to understand and straight forward fashion. (102 Pages) $14.95

Bigwig Briefs: Guerrilla Marketing
The Best of Guerrilla Marketing

Best selling author Jay Levinson shares the now world famous principles behind guerrilla marketing, in the first ever "brief" written on the subject. Items discussed include the Principles Behind Guerrilla Marketing, What Makes a Guerrilla, Attacking the Market, Everyone Is a Marketer, Media Matters, Technology and the Guerrilla Marketer, and Dollars and Sense. A must have for any big time marketing executive, small business owner, entrepreneur, marketer, advertiser, or any one interested in the amazing, proven power of guerrilla marketing. (102 Pages) $14.95

Other Best Selling Business Books Include:

ASPATORE
BUSINESS REVIEW

The Quarterly Book Featuring Excerpts From the Best Business Books

Aspatore Business Review is the perfect way for busy professionals to stay on top of the most pressing business issues. Each *Aspatore Business Review* includes knowledge excerpts and highlights from best selling business books, in-depth interviews with leading executives, and special features on emerging issues in the workplace. Every quarter, *Aspatore Business Review* brings you the most important excerpts from the best business books on topics such as:

- Management and Leadership
- Technology and the Internet
- Team Building
- Financial Accountability
- Staying ahead of Changing Markets
- Fostering Innovation
- Brand Building

Aspatore Business Review is the one book every business professional should read, and is the best way to keep current with your business reading in the most time efficient manner possible.

Subscribe Today to Aspatore Business Review
Fill Out the Order Form on the Other Side or Visit Us Online!

www.Aspatore.com

ASPATORE

BUSINESS REVIEW

Tear Out This Page and Mail or Fax To:

Aspatore Books, PO Box 883, Bedford, MA 01730
or
Fax to (617) 249-1970

Name:

Email:

Shipping Address:

City: State: Zip:

Billing Address:

City: State: Zip:

Phone:

(If mailing in a check you can skip this section but please read fine print below)
Credit Card Type (Visa & Mastercard ONLY):

Credit Card Number:

Expiration Date:

Signature:

*(Please note the billing address much match the address on file with your credit card company exactly)

Please make sure to provide your email address!
We shall send a confirmation receipt to your email address. Total charges for a full year of Aspatore Business Review are $109. If ordering from Massachusetts, please add 5% sales tax on the order (not including shipping and handling). If ordering from outside of the US, an additional $21.95 will be charged for shipping and handling costs. All books are paperback and will be shipped as soon as they become available. Sorry, no returns or refunds. Books that are not already published will be shipped upon publication date. Publication dates are subject to delay. For the most up to date information on publication dates and availability please visit www.Aspatore.com.

Bigwig Briefs
Condensed Business Intelligence From Industry Insiders

Become a Part of
Bigwig Briefs

Publish a Knowledge Excerpt on an Upcoming Topic (50-5,000 words), Submit an Idea to Write an Entire Bigwig Brief, Become a Reviewer, Post Comments on the Topics Mentioned, Read Expanded Excerpts, Free Excerpts From Upcoming Briefs

www.BigwigBriefs.com

Bigwig Briefs features condensed business intelligence from industry insiders and are the best way for business professionals to stay on top of the most pressing issues. There are two types of *Bigwig Briefs* books: the first is a compilation of excerpts from various executives on a topic, while the other is a book written solely by one individual on a specific topic. *Bigwig Briefs* is also the first interactive book series for business professionals whereby individuals can submit excerpts (50 to 5,000 words) for upcoming briefs on a topic they are knowledgeable on (submissions must be accepted by our editorial review committee and if accepted they receive a free copy of the book) or submit an idea to write an entire Bigwig Brief (accepted ideas/manuscripts receive a standard royalty deal). Bigwig Briefs is revolutionizing the business book market by providing the highest quality content, written by leading executives, in the most condensed format possible for business book readers worldwide.

**ASPATORE
BOOKS**